Lessons from Elijah

by

Andrew Wommack

Harrison House

23 22 21 20   10 9 8 7 6 5 4 3

Lessons from Elijah

ISBN: 978-160683-887-7

Copyright © 2013 by Andrew Wommack Ministries

P.O. Box 3333

Colorado Springs, CO 80934-3333

Published by:

Harrison House Publishers

Shippensburg, PA 17257

Table of Contents

Foreword

Most people learn much of what they know through the school of hard knocks. I've certainly attended that school. If you live through the hard lessons of your own mistakes, it makes a great testimony. But there is a better way.

Paul said in 1 Corinthians 10:6-11, "Now these things were our examples, to the intent we should not lust after evil things, as they also lusted. Neither be ye idolaters, as were some of them; as it is written, The people sat down to eat and drink, and rose up to play. Neither let us commit fornication, as some of them committed, and fell in one day three and twenty thousand. Neither let us tempt Christ, as some of them also tempted, and were destroyed of serpents. Neither murmur ye, as some of them also murmured, and were destroyed of the destroyer. Now all these things happened unto them for ensamples: and they are written for our admonition, upon whom the ends of the world are come."

Twice Paul made the point that all the things written in the Old Testament were for our example, that we might learn through them. It's better to learn through the mistakes of others than through our own.

I received the Lord at the age of eight and have been seeking the Lord my whole life. I haven't rebelled against God or experimented with many things that some reading this book have. That doesn't make me any better than anyone else, but in the eyes of some, it makes me less.

I've been told that you can't really know the goodness of God unless you've plumbed the depths of Satan's bondage. I beg to differ. Our Heavenly Father doesn't want us to learn the hard way, anymore than we want our children to suffer so they can better appreciate the good things of life. We can learn by the revelation of the Holy Spirit. That is why the Lord was so candid in sharing the strengths and weaknesses of His servants in the Bible. These things were written for our instruction.

Elijah is one of those Bible characters that the Lord has used to teach me some great lessons. Some of the things he did inspire me to believe God for more, while others serve as a constant reminder that apart from my faith in the Lord, I am and can do nothing (John 15:5). Elijah has been a mentor to me, although he lived thousands of years ago. Through scripture, his life has impacted me big time.

I pray that as I share some of the lessons I've learned from the Lord through Elijah, you too will open your heart and let the Holy Spirit teach you things that can inspire you to trust the Lord and make a difference as Elijah did. Through the story of Elijah, the Lord will also warn you about the pitfalls that brought Elijah down and show you how his faith allowed him to recover and become one of only two people in the Bible who never died. So join the class, open your heart, and let the Holy Spirit teach you lessons through the life of Elijah that will change you forever!

Chapter One

A Word from God

In 1 Kings 17, Elijah appears on the scene with no introduction. We are not told about his family history or how he came to know the Lord. The Bible just says that he was a Tishbite, which means he was an inhabitant of Gilead. "And Elijah the Tishbite, who was of the inhabitants of Gilead, said unto Ahab, As the LORD God of Israel liveth, before whom I stand, there shall not be dew nor rain these years, but according to my word" (1 Kings 17:1).

This scripture doesn't give Elijah any introduction. He just appears and gives the king a word from the Lord. There is no indication in Scripture that Elijah knew King Ahab or had any political clout or special access to him. In fact, just the opposite is implied.

Ahab and his wife, Jezebel, had been systematically killing all the prophets of the Lord (1 Kings 18:13). They fed 450 prophets of Baal and 400 prophets of the groves at their expense each day (1 Kings 18:19). They were trying to stamp out the worship of the true God of Israel in favor of the pagan worship of Baal. Elijah put his life at risk by coming to Ahab with a word from the Lord. This immediately identified him as one of the Lord's prophets and put him squarely in the crosshairs of Ahab and his wicked wife, Jezebel. The only thing that made Elijah stand out from everyone else was the fact that God had spoken to him; he had a word from God.

The leadership of the nation had instituted Baal worship and people were afraid to speak about their faith in the Lord. In many ways, it was very similar to what we see happening today. It is now "politically incorrect" to be committed to the Lord and have biblical standards. We may not be killed as they were in Elijah's day, but the persecution is still very real. Many believers are cowed into submission just as the people of Elijah's day were. But praise God that there was a man who had a word from God that penetrated the darkness of that day. Elijah had been in communion with the King of kings, so he went boldly into the presence of King Ahab and announced that there would be a drought for years until he said differently.

Where did Elijah get the boldness to do this? He could have been killed or imprisoned. What made Elijah fearless in the presence of the world's opposition? It was the word he had from God. Jeremiah 5:14 says, "Wherefore thus saith the LORD God of hosts, Because ye speak this word, behold, I will make my words in thy mouth fire, and this people wood, and it shall devour them." Jeremiah also said in Jeremiah 20:9, "But his word was in mine heart as a burning fire shut up in my bones, and I was weary with forbearing, and I could not stay."

God's Word is powerful (Hebrews 4:12). It's like a fire that devours anything in its path. It's also like a hammer that breaks into pieces everything that opposes it (Jeremiah 23:29). Anyone with a word from God is never inferior to those who don't have a word from the Lord.

Incorruptible Seed

Elijah had a word from God. He believed it enough to march boldly into the very presence of the king and declare, "There's going to be a drought according to my word." That's awesome!

You may be thinking, *I wish I had a word from the Lord.* You do! You have millions of words from the Lord in your Bible. You can't get saved without a word from God. It's the seed, the sperm of God's Word, that produced your new birth. That seed came to you as you heard and believed God's Word (Romans 10:17). "Being born again, not of corruptible seed, but of incorruptible, by the word of God, which liveth and abideth for ever" (1 Peter 1:23).

We have a word, or revelation, from God's Word. It's not a lack of words from God that is the problem; it's the failure of people to realize what they have in God's Word and act on it that is the problem today. You weren't born again by "accident." God's Word was literally planted in your heart, and that incorruptible, eternal seed—the same Word that spoke the worlds into existence—created a new creature on the inside of you. God's Word germinated and exploded in your heart.

Every true believer has a word from God. We just haven't fully recognized and truly understood what we have. We have allowed the world and the fear of man to intimidate us (Proverbs 29:25), and make us feel like we're the ones who are weird for being moral and having convictions. The world labels us as "bigots" or "prejudiced," because we believe that some things are absolute. We're the ones who have the revelation of God's Word. The problem is we just aren't as bold with that revelation as Elijah was.

Straight to the Top

What would have happened if Elijah had just stayed in his prayer closet and only *prayed* concerning the word that God had spoken to him about the drought? What would have happened if he had never gone and spoken to the king? I'm not sure there would have been a drought if Elijah hadn't spoken forth and acted on the word God gave him. Even if the drought had come, King Ahab wouldn't have recognized it as being from the hand of God. He would have rationalized and written it off as circumstance and coincidence.

Elijah took what the Lord had said to him and boldly spoke it when there wasn't any physical proof that it would come to pass. It was really easy for the king to just reject Elijah's message and say, "Who are you and what makes your word more important than anyone else's?" Although Ahab blew off Elijah's message and forgot about it at first, as the drought manifested over time... "... There **[was]** no nation or kingdom, whither **[King Ahab]** hath not sent to seek **[Elijah]**: and when they said, He is not **[here]**; he took an oath of the kingdom and nation, that they found **[him]** not" (1 Kings 18:10; brackets mine).

Elijah's boldness to go and speak forth the word is what made everything else begin to happen. That's what set his whole ministry in motion. All of the great miracles—multiplying food, calling down fire from heaven, raising the dead, etc.—began with him getting a word about a drought and just being bold enough to go straight to the very top! He went right into the presence of the king and spoke what God had given him.

No Substitute

Boldly speaking forth and acting upon the Word of God in faith will set your life and ministry in motion. It doesn't matter if salvation, Holy Spirit baptism, or healing is all you have. The average person doesn't know that. You're passing people every day of your life who don't have a clue about things on which you have a word from God. But you have to speak up to make a difference.

Today, many people have substituted prayer for speaking forth and acting on God's Word. I'm not against prayer. In fact, I'm all for it—in its proper place. However, Elijah could have prayed over the word he received from God from then until Jesus came, but nothing would have happened if he hadn't been bold enough to go speak the word and act on it in faith and obedience.

Elijah came on the scene with no introduction. He didn't have a genealogy, an education, or a degree. All he had was the Word of God, and that was all he needed. The devil will try to make you think you just don't have enough. I certainly had to deal with that. I was just like Jeremiah who said, "Ah, Lord GOD! behold, I cannot speak: for I [am] a child" (Jeremiah 1:6). I was an introverted hick from Texas. I thought, *How could God ever use me?* But then I discovered His Word and found out it is God's Word that produces the fruit (Mark 4:14-20). I'm just the dirt the seed is planted in. I don't make a good seed, but I'm good dirt.

If God has given you a revelation of His nature and character, you have something that will put you over the top. If the Lord has shown you any truth—spoken anything to you—then you have something that will ignite miracles if you're bold enough to act on that word and speak it!

The Next Step

"**And the word of the LORD came unto him,saying**, Get thee hence, and turn thee eastward, and hide thyself by the brook Cherith, that is before Jordan. And it shall be, that thou shalt drink of the brook; and I have commanded the ravens to feed thee there" (1 Kings 17:2-4; emphasis mine).

God didn't show Elijah the outcome ahead of time. He didn't receive the word about God supernaturally supplying his need and protecting him at the brook Cherith until after he had acted on the first word the Lord gave him. Elijah didn't know everything that was going to happen. He didn't know he was going to multiply the widow's food (1 Kings 17:14-16), raise her son from the dead (1 Kings 17:17-23), and call down fire out of heaven (1 Kings 18:37-38). He didn't know that a great revival was coming (1 Kings 18:39).

Elijah didn't have foreknowledge of the end result. Scripture reveals that this second word concerning his direction, protection, and provision (1 Kings 17:2-4) came <u>after</u> he had already been bold and stepped out in faith on the previous word (1 Kings 17:1). Have you ever experienced this in your life? I have! When we receive a word from God, we usually allow our mind to go ahead and think, *Okay, now how's this going to work? If I do this, then what's going to happen over here?* We try to figure it all out. We want to have the entire picture before we step out on God's Word. Elijah didn't have that! He didn't know that the Lord was going to make supernatural provision for him. He just had one word from God: "Tell the king a drought is coming." Then after he was faithful to go and speak forth that word, God revealed the next step.

There are steps and stages to walking with God. One of the things that hinder us from really seeing His best in our lives is wanting to get the end result before stepping out in faith on the word we already have. We want to play it safe and say, "Lord, if I do this, then what will You do? How will You provide all of my needs? Will everything work out?" However, the Lord doesn't usually work that way.

Elijah just had one word from God. He stepped out and spoke it. He went straight to the king, without any guarantee of protection. According to Scripture, all the Lord showed him was that there was going to be a drought (1 Kings 17:1). It wasn't until after he spoke that word that the Lord came to him with this promise of protection, direction, and provision.

Act On It

We're playing it too safe! We have to get out and do what God has told us to do. We need to act on the word we have before we get another one. Every once in a while, I catch myself looking at our Bible college students and thinking, *Man, they haven't got a chance! They'll never make it! That person doesn't even have enough sense to get out of town.* Yet they have all this zeal and a word from God.

Just about the time I'm tempted to tell them, "You'll never make it," the Lord reminds me that I didn't have a clue what was going on when I got started either. But we *did* have a word from God. Jamie and I jumped out and did things that I wouldn't encourage anybody to do. It makes a great testimony if you live through it, but not many people do!

When Jamie and I were first married, I had about $3,000. I cashed it all in and turned it into $100 bills. In one week's time, I gave it all away because I was so excited about getting out there and seeing God meet our needs supernaturally. That's stupid! That's dumb to the second power, or "dumb dumb."

Even though this definitely isn't the way to do it, my heart attitude was right. I was actually anticipating the challenge and genuinely looking forward to believing God. I knew it would take a miracle for the Lord to fulfill His word to me, and I was excited to get started! I had zeal, but very little knowledge.

After going through some things, you realize how stupid you've been and you start trying to act smarter. There is no premium on ignorance, but if you aren't careful, you'll become so cautious that you won't listen for the voice of God and step out in faith anymore. Yet a person with a word from God will beat a smart person every time.

There needs to be a balance. You need enthusiasm and zeal, but it should be tempered with wisdom and knowledge. If you aren't careful, you will get to a place where you won't do anything until God has already planned it out, shown you the end result, and accounted for everything that could possibly happen. Elijah got a word from God, stepped out, and spoke it. He didn't have a clue what was going to happen next. He didn't have a plan, but he did have a word from God!

Maybe the Lord has shown you something or has done something and spoken into your life. You are praying and asking Him to show you more, but He's saying, "Act on it!" When you step out and begin doing something with what God has already called you to do, that's when the miracles start happening!

The Lord won't show you steps two through ten until you've acted on step one. Why would He show you more if you haven't already done what He told you to do? That would just make you accountable for more if you fail. He just shows you one step at a time because He loves you so much.

The Lord told us to pray for our daily bread (Matthew 6:11), not a year's supply of food. However, most of us would prefer to get it all at one time. It doesn't take any faith to live that way. We just believe the Lord once and then go on our merry way. The Lord wants us to be totally dependent on Him. He shows us His will and His way one step at a time, and only after we act on that does He give us our next instructions.

Are you acting on the word you already have from the Lord?

Chapter Two

A Place Called "There"

Further direction came to Elijah, along with the promise of protection and provision, after he stepped out in faith and acted on the initial word he had been given. "And the word of the Lord came unto him, saying, Get thee hence, and turn thee eastward, and hide thyself by the brook Cherith, that is before Jordan. And it shall be, that thou shalt drink of the brook; and I have commanded the ravens to feed thee **there**" (1 Kings 17:2-4; emphasis mine).

God made supernatural provision for Elijah. As you can imagine, Elijah was in trouble with the king once the word about the drought actually started to come to pass. Ahab began to look for him, so God hid, protected, and provided for him during this period of time. Notice where the Lord sent this provision: "I have commanded the ravens to feed thee **there**" (1 Kings 17:4; emphasis mine). God made provision for Elijah, but it wasn't sent directly to him. The provision was sent "there"—to the place the Lord told him to go.

God Always Provides

Whenever God tells you to do something, He makes full provision for you. There's always an ample supply for anything the Lord tells you to do. Yet, I've seen people who have stepped out on a word from God and didn't see everything work out. Instead of seeing the provision, they suffered many problems instead. This makes you wonder, if you're honest and bold enough to admit it, *What happened to these folks? Was God faithful?*

God sent the supply to where He told Elijah to go—not to where he was. He didn't send the provision to Elijah directly. He sent provision to the Brook Cherith. I'm not exactly sure how God speaks to ravens, but He didn't send them to where Elijah was. He must have given them a grid coordinate somewhere along the Brook Cherith and told them to take the food there.

The supply was sent where God told Elijah to go. If he had stayed right where he was, the Lord still would have supplied the food because verse four says, "I HAVE commanded the ravens …" The Lord had already spoken to the birds instructing them to take the food for Elijah. It would be there, even if Elijah wasn't. God's provision wasn't dependent on Elijah's obedience, but Elijah's ability to receive God's provision was.

Those ravens were going to bring bread and flesh every morning and evening and pile it high beside the water. Yet, if Elijah had failed to go where God told him to go, he could have starved to death while wondering, *God, where are You? I stepped out on Your Word, but where's Your supply?*

God provides for us every single time. He loves us and has made abundant provision for everything we need, but that provision isn't sent to where we are. It's sent to where we're supposed to be. Therefore, if we aren't obedient and don't follow through on what He has told us to do, we can miss His supply.

Go Deep

When a quarterback throws a pass to his receiver, he doesn't throw the football to where the receiver is; he throws it to where the receiver is supposed to be. I've watched quarterbacks throw the football long before the receiver makes his break. The receiver may even be headed in the opposite direction from where he eventually catches the ball. But the quarterback and the receiver have made prior arrangements. They have called a play in which the ball will be thrown to a specific spot, and in order for the receiver to make the catch, he has to run to that specific spot. That's why you will sometimes see the ball thrown to a place where there's no one. You might wonder, *What was the quarterback thinking? No one was even near the ball. Either the quarterback or the receiver made a mistake.*

Never forget, the Lord is the one calling the plays in our lives. He sends our provision to where He tells us to go, not to where we are. If we make a wrong turn or don't ever move off the line of scrimmage, we aren't going to receive. And it's not the Lord's fault.

He's always faithful to give, but we have to be in the right place to receive.

It's Proportional

When Jamie and I first started out in ministry, I did many things wrong. This hindered our finances and our ability to receive God's provision. For at least five years, we were constantly on the edge of starving to death. There was literally just a step between us and death all the time. Here we were preaching the Gospel—speaking of abundant life and prosperity—yet we were suffering. Since things weren't working in our personal lives. I had to constantly battle thoughts like, *God, it's not working. You aren't faithful. I'm doing what You told me to do, but where's the supply?*

Looking back now, I can see all the different ways I was violating the Word. We were told, "If you're called to be a minister then you're sinning against God if you do anything but minister. If you get a job, you're denying your call. You aren't faithful!" Due to this misconception, I just committed myself to full-time ministry no matter what.

The first church we pastored in Segoville, Texas, only had about eight to ten people in attendance. Yet, we were having five services a week. I refused to work another job because I was "called," and I was determined to be "faithful." As a result, I hindered my own finances. Later, the Lord showed me that His provision is proportional. "Even so hath the Lord ordained that they which preach the gospel should live of the gospel" (1 Corinthians 9:14).

When you are ministering full time, you can expect to live off the Gospel full time. But if ten people are all you're ministering to right now, you ought to get a job. It's not wrong to supplement your income. You're not denying your call. It's wisdom to do something else to help support yourself and your family. It took me years to get this through my thick skull!

We survived, but the provision that God really had for us was "over there." It was somewhere else. It wouldn't be found in the way I was walking. I had a pure heart but a dumb head. I wasn't doing what the Word said. God was making provision. As a matter of fact, several people offered me jobs that would have fit in my schedule so I could still pastor and minister. This was God's provision, but I refused to receive it because I thought I would be sinning against my calling if I got a job. I made a mistake. My teachings entitled *Blessings & Miracles* and *Financial Stewardship* will help you understand how to receive God's abundant supply and avoid making the same mistakes I made.

Obedience Matters

There's a place called "there" for every one of us. You can't necessarily see it from where you are. You just have to step out in faith on what God has told you to do. The provision isn't where you are. It's "there"—it's found while you're out doing what God has told you to do. Many people are waiting to see the provision before they step out, but God said, "I have already commanded the ravens to feed you there!"

The Brook Cherith must have been at least two or three miles long. How did Elijah know which spot to camp at along the brook? He knew he was in the right place because God had already spoken to the ravens, and they could certainly fly there quicker than he could walk. Therefore, he knew he was in the right place when he saw the provision of bread and flesh. God had already sent the provision. All Elijah had to do was obey. "So he went and did according unto the word of the LORD" (1 Kings 17:5).

Obedience matters! God gave Elijah a word. He knew there was going to be a need in Elijah's life for protection and supernatural supply, so God made the provision and sent the ravens. What would have happened if Elijah hadn't obeyed? God's provision would have just lay there rotting, and Elijah could have starved. There is a place for obedience. Obedience doesn't change God's heart toward you, but if you aren't obedient, you can certainly make it hard on yourself.

God has a purpose for you. He has put a call on your life. Supernatural provision has already been sent to accomplish whatever God has told you to do, but it's "there." The problem is that we aren't all "there" yet! We're doing our own thing, in our own timing, and in our own way. But there is an anointing on being obedient to God and doing what He says.

Pritchett, Colorado

After struggling for most of the first ten years of our ministry, we finally began to see a small measure of success in the second place I pastored, Childress, Texas. About fifty people attended our church and for the first time in my life, there was light at the end of the tunnel—and it wasn't another train! I was excited! We were eating regularly for the first time, and things were beginning to work out. Great miracles happened and this small measure of success took a little bit of the pressure off.

During this period of time, Don Krow's sister and brother-in-law asked us to come up to Colorado Springs to minister. On our way, we stopped to see a friend of ours in Kim, Colorado—a tiny old town of eighty people in the middle of nowhere. As we visited with them, they invited us to come and minister in the Bible study they had in Pritchett, Colorado.

I thought, *Sure, I'll go minister anywhere.*

I remember driving through Pritchett with the Krows. We started laughing and saying, "Who would want to live in this dippy place?" Jokingly I stated, "Don, I believe God is calling you to Pritchett, Colorado!" Ironically, within a few weeks, the people of Pritchett asked me to come and hold a meeting. During this meeting, we saw a man raised from the dead. It turned that church upside down! Pritchett only had about 144 residents, 10 of whom attended this church.

When I was ready to leave, they sat me down and said, "You've come here and destroyed everything we ever believed. We've experienced the power of God, and you're just going to waltz in and out of here in a week and leave us? You can't do this! God is calling you to Pritchett, Colorado!"

I laughed as I replied, "You must be kidding!" However, by the time I arrived home, the Lord had spoken to me to go to Pritchett, Colorado.

We went there out of sheer obedience, believing that Pritchett was our "there." It was where God had called us to be. We didn't expect anything in return, but that's where our ministry exploded. That's where everything took off. That's where God began to pour out His blessing.

We didn't take an offering or a salary from the church. The church grew from just a few people to a hundred in just a very short period of time. We were only there six months, but our ministry income increased to $6,000 a month. We prospered as never before!

That's where God opened up both our radio and tape ministry. That's where our whole ministry started. We just took a step of obedience to go "there." Nobody in his right mind would have ever thought that Pritchett was "there" for anyone! But that's where God told me to go. I believe God has something like that for everyone's life.

Your Provision Is "There"

The Lord asked Abraham to sacrifice his son. That didn't make sense. It looked like he was killing the promise, but that was "there" for him. It was what God called him to do.

You can look at all the major characters in the Bible and see that God asked just about every single one of them to do something completely illogical. Yet, what He was looking for was just an act of obedience. That's where the supernatural power of God comes into play. You can probably think of something like this that the Lord has asked you to do. That's just how He operates!

God has already sent your provision "there." If you're missing out on His supernatural supply, it's because you aren't "there." You aren't doing what you know in your heart God has called you to do. Even when you step out, take a risk, throw caution to the wind, and do everything God tells you to do, it will still often take a great miracle to see something happen. It's still hard! But if you aren't even doing what you know in your heart God has called you to do, then you don't stand a chance at experiencing success.

Hearing from God and acting on that word is simply a necessity if you ever want to see His power manifest in your life. The Lord will never do anything to destroy you. He might do a few things to test you, but He'll never do anything to hurt you. There's a tremendous blessing and anointing in being "there" and doing what God has called you to do. Are you "there?" If not, why not? Do what the Lord tells you to do.

Chapter Three
Natural & Supernatural

Your place called "there" isn't necessarily a specific geographic location. It's often more an attitude of wholeheartedly moving toward doing what God has said for you to do. "So he went and did according unto the word of the Lord: for he went and dwelt by the brook Cherith, that is before Jordan. And the ravens brought him bread and flesh in the morning, and bread and flesh in the evening; and he drank of the brook" (1 Kings 17:5-6).

There was a supernatural supply of bread and flesh, but there was also a natural supply of water. The water wasn't a supernatural supply. It was already there and had been for thousands of years. It was natural.

When God calls you to do something, the provision is not totally supernatural. There are also natural things that will meet your needs. I got in trouble in my early years because I had been led to believe that since the Lord had called me into the ministry, He was going to meet all my needs supernaturally. I was just expecting God to rain money out of heaven. I refused to take any natural action, like working. I was trying to be all spiritual, while rejecting the natural provision God might send. But God's supply is both supernatural and natural.

You need to keep things in balance. You'll find yourself in a ditch if you're always looking for your needs to be met in a totally natural, human way. When you do this, you look to yourself and the pressure is on you to provide. In the same way, you'll find yourself in a ditch if you just expect God to rain down provision out of heaven while you refuse to do anything according to natural wisdom.

100 x 0 = 0

We led a Baptist pastor into the baptism in the Holy Spirit. He became so excited about the Lord that he was kicked out of the Baptist church. He started coming to our church, but he wouldn't work because he was so fanatical about believing God to meet his needs in a supernatural way. By this time, the Lord had shown me these things, so I was trying to teach him that it's okay to go out and work a job even though he's called to the ministry. This guy was starving!

One day I told him, "The Bible says the Lord will bless the work of your hands. A hundred times zero equals zero (100 x 0 = 0). Do something, even if it's just a little. Go get a job at the burger joint, but do something and God will prosper it."

He replied, "Well, back when I was in the world, I used to fix dents and upholstery on cars. If I ever needed work, I'd just take one of my business cards, go downtown, and find a vehicle that had a ding in it. If it would normally cost $100 to fix the ding, I'd give them a twenty-five percent discount and bid the job for $75. I'd stick my business card with the bid written on the back of it in the door. By nightfall, I'd have four or five jobs."

I asked, "Well, why don't you do that now?"

"I'm waiting on God to meet my needs," he responded.

I told him, "God can meet your needs through that skill."

Finally, I convinced him and he started sticking his business card in the doors of dinged up cars and the money started coming in. The Lord began prospering him. He did a natural thing with the supernatural blessing of God upon it. Sometimes people have trouble understanding this interaction between the natural and the supernatural.

A Timely Tithe

At one point in time, the board of Andrew Wommack Ministries told me, "It's over. Turn out the lights. Quit!" As we were just sitting around trying to figure out what to do because, on paper, we were bankrupt, my mother called from the office and told me that an offering of $60,000 had just come in from a church! We started rejoicing!

The board told me, "Don't spend it until you make sure the check clears the bank." It cleared just fine—praise God! It turned out that this gift was from a little church in Kansas that I had never been to before or since. This church of two or three hundred people didn't know my need, but they sent me an offering of $60,000. You're probably thinking, *That was just totally supernatural.*

It was definitely God, but it wasn't just "totally" supernatural. The fellow who started that church had attended one of our camp meetings several years earlier. By a gift of the Holy Spirit, I called him out and prophesied over him some things that were going to happen and I told him that God had called him to the pastorate. After receiving that prophecy, he went into the ministry and went home and started a church.

Four or five years later, he led a man to the Lord in his church who was a millionaire. After being born again, this man gave him something like $150,000 or $200,000. The man said, "This is my tithe. I don't know where it's supposed to go. Would you please tithe it for me?"

Ever since I spoke that word into the pastor's life at our camp meeting by the insight of the Holy Spirit, he had wanted to bless me back. I sowed seed into his life several years before, so he sent me $60,000 as the Lord enabled him to do so. So you see, this timely provision from God was both natural and supernatural.

A Combination of the Two

One of my partners is a big giver, but he's always on my case saying, "If you have a need, don't put out a letter or tell anybody. Just pray to God and He will supernaturally meet your need." That sounds great, but that's not the way things work. The Word says, "Ye have not, because ye ask not" (James 4:2).

God told Moses to take an offering from the children of Israel and Moses was to tell them to give specific things (Exodus 25:1-7). It's wrong to just expect God's provision to be one hundred percent supernatural. However, it's also wrong to get out there and try to figure it all out in the physical realm. God will tell you natural things to do, but there will also be a supernatural supply.

Elijah had supernatural bread and meat, but he also had natural water. It was a combination of the two. You can't live without water. Neither can you live one hundred percent on the supernatural. There are some carnal, natural things you must do also.

Natural Wisdom

One of the best things that happened to our ministry came in the form of natural wisdom. One of my partners has a business that grosses about $550 million a year. About four or five years ago, he brought his accountant into our ministry to look things over. After a couple of days the accountant said, "Something is wrong. On paper, you're bankrupt. Yet, you aren't. You're still functioning and things are working. We're just going to have to go through everything from the top to the bottom and check things out."

One of the main things they found was nearly $200,000 worth of inventory sitting in a back room. Since products like our *Life for Today* study Bibles were less expensive to buy in bulk, I purchased large quantities of them. Instead of paying $10 for each Bible, we only paid $5. But that meant we had something like $60,000 worth of Bibles just sitting there. When the accountant saw this, he started teaching me about something called "Just-in-Time Management." He said, "You have money just sitting there in that storage room that could be out paying bills and other things." So we bled our inventory down to bare bones. Since then, we haven't had a financial crisis in our ministry.

That was just natural wisdom; it wasn't supernatural. Yet, sometimes we look for everything to be just totally supernatural. Now don't misunderstand me, we all need the supernatural power of God, but there are also some natural things that we have to do in cooperation with God.

Chapter Four

"There" Changes

"And it came to pass after a while, that the brook dried up, because there had been no rain in the land" (1 Kings 17:7). Just because God gave you a word, you obeyed it, and He supernaturally provided for you, doesn't mean the word won't ever change! "There" is not a static place. At times, it's going to change.

Dynamic & Progressive

There are progressive steps toward the fulfillment of anything God has for you to do. "First the blade, then the ear, after that the full corn in the ear" (Mark 4:28). Many people are stuck in the same place they were five, ten, or even twenty years ago. They seek God when their back is against the wall, when they're desperate and nothing is going right. Then He opens up a door and they start getting some relief. They begin to see the power of God and experience some success, but then they let up and over time, they slide back to where they were before.

The Christian life is a relationship. It's dynamic and progressive. At times, God is going to change some things in your life. Will you continue following Him or not? Will you go on to the new "there" or get stuck?

No Problems?

For a period of time, God sent Elijah's supply to the Brook Cherith. However, the brook dried up after a while "because there had been no rain in the land" (1 Kings 7:7). Can you guess why there wasn't any rain in the land? That's right! It was because Elijah had received, proclaimed, and obeyed the word of the Lord. It wasn't because he had done anything wrong. The brook dried up because he did things right. Sometimes we think we will never have any problems if we just do what God tells us to do, but this just isn't so!

Consider Paul. He was led by a heavenly vision to go to Macedonia (Acts 16:9-10). First thing in the morning, he got up and went there. Paul assumed that surely the Lord had sent them to preach the Gospel in Philippi (a city in the province of Macedonia). He wasn't there forty-eight hours before he was thrown into the worst part of the prison (Acts 16:22-24). His obedience to God to go "there" and do what He told him to do caused him problems.

Facing Opposition

It's wrong to think that if you're doing what God wants you to do, then you will never have to face any opposition or problems. However, the vast majority of believers functionally interpret whether or not they're doing what the Lord wants them to do by how easy their life is. If something comes against them, they think they've missed God.

If you follow that logic, then Abraham, Isaac, Joseph, and Moses all missed God. Moses obeyed the Lord and went back to Egypt. He threw his rod down in front of Pharaoh and commanded, "Let my people go!" Instead of the Israelites being set free, things became worse. Pharaoh doubled their work and took away their straw. The people wanted to kill Moses. Everything became worse, not better.

Joseph acted on the word God gave him. Instead of things getting better, he was beaten, thrown into a pit, nearly killed, and sold into slavery. While a slave, he was faithful and obeyed God. But just as things were starting to improve, his master's wife lied about him and he found himself in prison again. Every time he obeyed God, it looked like things got worse. But all along the way, the Lord had His hand on Joseph.

The Word describes Joseph, a slave standing naked on the auction block, as "a prosperous man" (Genesis 39:2). Nobody in the natural would have considered him a prosperous man at that moment in his life, but he was obeying God. He was standing steadfastly in that place called "there." Even in prison, "God was with him" (Acts 7:9). Later, Joseph prospered and became the head of the prison. God's blessing and anointing will be on your life when you're really obeying Him, but that doesn't mean that everything in the physical realm will be going right.

When All Hell Has Broken Loose

I was with Bob and Joy Nichols when the doctor walked in and said, "Your daughter is dead. Pull the plug. She's brain dead." The doctor was polite, but his prognosis was the total opposite of the word Bob and Joy had from the Lord.

Bob didn't get mad. He just sweetly, kindly, and lovingly told the doctor, "No, that's not what we're believing." Their daughter is now at home recovering. She's been on a treadmill, talks a little bit, and continues improving day by day.

I've known pastors who had people almost split their church, but they just blessed them and sent them out. Rather than letting these people divide their fellowship, they sowed them and encouraged them on their way. We think we have problems until we hear what other folks have been through. In the midst of opposition and pain, their joy, peace, and victory challenges us to also rise up in faith.

This idea that if God is blessing and you're really succeeding, there will be no opposition, isn't true. In fact, the opposite is actually true. You can sometimes tell whether or not God is in what you're doing by how much opposition you face. Neither way is one hundred percent correct all the time. You need to have a word from God to know for sure. But if you were going to look at it in the natural, it's probably more scriptural to say that you're in the right place when all hell has broken loose and everything is going against you. That's about the way it goes in Scripture.

Wait for the New Word

Here Elijah was—he knew that he was in the blessing of God. He was in that place called "there." He was obeying God, but the brook dried up. And worse yet, he's the one who caused it to do that! It was his own prophecy that brought the drought. It was his own preaching that got him into the mess he was in. Elijah is proof that you can preach yourself into a corner.

To Elijah's credit, however, he didn't move just because the brook dried up. This was a serious situation because he needed water to live. You can only go three days without water before you begin to die. Seven days without water and you're dead. You can go forty days without food, but you can't go without water very long.

In a situation like this, when the supply has quit and something has to change, most people wouldn't wait on a word from God. They would feel like they had to do something, and they would act out of panic. There have been so many times in our ministry when it looked like the end was near, and I didn't know what to do. I prayed and asked God, but I didn't have a new word. I didn't have any different instruction than what I was already doing. Everything in the natural was screaming, "You have to do something! You can't just sit there!" But really, until God speaks, you can't do anything else.

You couldn't expect Elijah to just sit there and die of thirst. He had to have water. God could have supplied the water supernaturally. Moses hit a rock and water gushed out, enough for all the Israelites and their cattle (Exodus 17:6). Samson nearly died of thirst. God gave him water from the jawbone of an ass (Judges 15:15-19). The precedent was already there for God to move supernaturally. Elijah didn't have to move to get his need met. God could have done it supernaturally.

Sometimes we just allow circumstances to dictate to us and say, *You have to do something—move!* But in truth, we don't ever have to do anything contrary to what the Lord has told us to do. If God gave you a word, then the thing to do is to keep doing what the Lord told you to do until you get a new word. You may say, "But Andrew, you can't always do that." Yes, you can!

Deal with Your Thoughts

One of my good friends, Pastor Bob Nichols, really struggled under some financial pressures with his church awhile back. He told a story about a time when he was facing a balloon payment on his church that was totally impossible to pay in the natural. It looked like everything he had believed for decades was done for. He was desperate.

He went out into a field one evening and said he wouldn't leave that field until he had a word from God. He spent all night out there without anything. It was beginning to get light outside and he felt like he had to leave because people would be able to see him there, so he got in his car and turned the ignition and the radio came on. He didn't realize it was the radio at first, because he had forgotten that he had left it on. The voice of Brother Shambach came on saying, "Preacher, you don't have any problem. All you need is faith in God."

Immediately Bob turned the car off. He thought this was the Lord speaking to him in an audible voice. But in just a few seconds, he realized what had happened. That realization, however, didn't change the impact those words had on him. God had spoken to him through that voice. He had a word from God and sure enough, it all worked out. The church has now more than doubled its assets and they are debt free. Hallelujah! God is faithful!

Everybody runs across situations in which they know what God wants them to do, but it looks like they just can't do it. Circumstances won't allow them to do it and they feel like they need to bail out. Their decision in a situation like this will determine whether they really go on and see the blessing of God or not.

Elijah had to cooperate with God through this ordeal. If Elijah had run from there without getting a word from God, I believe the Lord wouldn't have spoken to him about Zarephath (1 Kings 17:9). Then all of the other things that happened in Elijah's ministry wouldn't have come to pass either.

The brook didn't just dry up all at once. It started having less and less and less water in it, until finally it got down to a trickle and stopped. Elijah could see this coming. We can usually see when we're getting into trouble and things aren't working out. Our biggest problem is our own thoughts about the situation. The Word doesn't tell us what Elijah was thinking, but apparently he was so committed to the fact that the Lord had told him to be there at the Brook Cherith, that he wasn't going to move until He heard from God again. Elijah just dealt with all his contrary thoughts.

He Leads You in Steps

"And the word of the LORD came unto him, saying, Arise get thee to Zarephath, which belongeth to Zidon, and dwell **there**: behold, I have commanded a widow woman **there** to sustain thee" (1 Kings 17:8-9; emphasis mine). God changed Elijah's "there." He changed the place of provision.

God leads us in steps. He called me to pastor for a period of time. This wasn't for the people I would help; it was for me. It was my time of training. Lord have mercy on those poor people who made up the congregations during those years when I was learning! God definitely led me to do what I was doing at the time, but if I had stopped there, I would have missed His real purpose for my life. God will lead you in stages.

I pastored three small churches over a six-year period of time. I thought that would be what I did forever. But then the Lord moved me into a radio and traveling ministry for the next twenty years, and I thought that's what I would do forever. Then the Lord told me to start a Bible college. That had been the farthest thing from my mind, but I did it, and it has proven to be one of the most important things the Lord has led me to do.

Next, the Lord gave me a word about going on television. As I prepared to take that step, the Lord spoke to me on July 26, 1999, and told me that I was just now beginning to do what He made me to do. Even though I had been in ministry for thirty-one years, if I had died before I began my TV ministry on January 3, 2000, I would have missed His will for my life.

Once I was on television, we saw tremendous growth in the ministry. But the Lord wasn't through. The second most significant encounter I've had with the Lord came on January 31, 2002. The Lord told me that my small thinking was limiting what He could do in my life and ministry. It was time to grow again. Almost immediately, the ministry just exploded with growth that continues to this day.

I have now been in full-time ministry for forty-five years. But I couldn't do what I'm doing now forty-five years ago. God grows you by steps as you learn to fulfill His will. Don't let what you don't know keep you from doing what you do know to do. As you take that first step, the Lord will be faithful to show you the following steps. That's my testimony, and that's what the Lord did for Elijah.

Chapter Five

"The" Widow Woman

God led Elijah to a new place. "Behold, I have commanded a widow woman there to sustain thee" (1 Kings 17:9). The Lord had already spoken to this widow, just as He had done with the ravens. He had already spoken to the ravens before He told Elijah about it (1 Kings 17:4). Likewise, God had already spoken to this woman.

This is important because this widow wasn't just anyone. Elijah wasn't just led by circumstances to the first person he ran into. God sent him to a *specific* woman. Jesus himself said, "But I tell you of a truth, many widows were in Israel in the days of Elias **[Elijah],** when the heaven was shut up three years and six months, when great famine was throughout all the land; but unto none of them was Elias sent, save unto Sarepta **[Zarephath]**, a city of Sidon, unto a woman that was a widow" (Luke 4:25-26; brackets mine).

God sent Elijah to this specific widow woman. Verse 9 reveals that God had already commanded her to sustain him. Perhaps she had heard about Elijah's prophecy and knew that this drought had been caused by the man of God. Perhaps she was believing the Lord would send Elijah her way, because she knew she was supposed to sustain him. It's also possible God showed her that somehow or another, He was going to miraculously provide for her through the drought. We don't know how detailed the message she received from God was, but we know the Lord had already spoken to her heart. He had already commanded this widow woman to sustain Elijah.

Miracles Take Two

"So he arose and went to Zarephath. And when he came to the gate of the city, behold, **the** widow woman…" (1 Kings 17:10; emphasis mine). This wasn't "a" widow woman Elijah encountered; it was "the" widow woman. If Elijah could hear God tell him, "Go to Zarephath. There is a widow there who will sustain you," then he could also hear Him say, "She's the one." Elijah knew this wasn't just any woman; she was "the" woman. "The widow woman was **there** gathering of sticks…" (1 Kings 17:10; emphasis mine). This widow woman was "there." God had a place called "there" for her too!

It takes two people for a miracle to happen. God had already told this woman that He was going to sustain her. She was out there picking up sticks. That's pretty mundane. She wasn't doing anything special. She wasn't out there praying, laying hands on the sick, or doing anything "holy." She was just picking up sticks so she could make a fire and cook her last little bit of food. This may not seem very significant, but she was "there."

Right Place, Right Time

Many people would have thought, had they been in the situation of this widow woman, *It's my last little bit of food. It's my last day. I give up!* They would have been back at their house griping, complaining, and quitting. They might have been depressed or desperately praying for God to do something. But this widow woman was just "there" doing what she knew to do. This put her in the right place at the right time.

Sometimes we want to do all these super-spiritual things. We want God to do something in a spectacular supernatural fashion. Yet, sometimes we encounter the most awesome miracles just doing the everyday things God has called us to do.

Abraham was sitting at his tent's door when the Lord appeared to him (Genesis 18:1). Jacob was asleep when the Lord spoke to him (Genesis 28:11-16). Moses was tending sheep when the Lord appeared to him (Exodus 3:1-2). Gideon was threshing wheat (Judges 6:11), Saul was looking for lost animals (1 Samuel 9). And David was watching his father's sheep (1 Samuel 16:11) when the Lord called him and anointed him to be king.

We could receive a word from the Lord while talking to people at the store, being kind to neighbors, or loving co-workers. The Word says that "some have entertained angels unawares" (Hebrews 13:2). Many of us are down at the church building looking for a heavenly vision or an angel to walk through the door, when the truth is we pass them on the street. If we aren't living the Christian life in everyday things, we could be missing out on God's blessing. We could miss out on our miracle because we are too spiritual!

If this woman hadn't been there just picking up sticks, which was really an insignificant thing, she could have missed her miracle. God has called you to do a lot of things that aren't necessarily super-spiritual. Sometimes we look down on those things and don't do them with as much joy as all the spiritual stuff. There are just some natural things that we need to do. Be faithful to do what God has called you to do. Remember, this woman was "there," picking up sticks when her chance for a miracle approached.

Serve Somebody

"And he called to her, and said, Fetch me, I pray thee, a little water in a vessel, that I may drink" (1 Kings 17:10). If you were getting ready to cook your last little bit of food and then die and somebody came to you and asked for a drink of water, would you give it to them? How about if both you and your refrigerator were full and everything looked good for you and a stranger came up to you and asked for a drink of water, would you give it to him? Many Christians would say, "Who died and made you God? Go get it yourself!"

For this woman to actually serve Elijah first says a lot about her. I believe that's one of the reasons why God chose her over everyone else to provide for His messenger. She was a giver. She was someone who didn't just think only of herself. Here she was on what seemed to be her last day on the face of the earth, yet she was willing to serve somebody. Many of us aren't willing to serve anybody on a good day, much less a bad one.

"And as she was going to fetch it, he called to her and said..." (1 Kings 17:11). Remember, Elijah knew this was "the" woman. He wasn't just asking her for assistance randomly to check her out. He was calling to her on purpose. "Bring me, I pray thee, a morsel of bread in thine hand. And she said, As the LORD thy God liveth, I have not a cake, but an handful of meal in a barrel, and a little oil in a cruse: and, behold, I am gathering two sticks, that I may go in and dress it for me and my son, that we may eat it, and die" (1 Kings 17:11-12).

Now that doesn't seem like a very positive confession. On the surface, it appears as if the woman is in total unbelief. Yet the Word reveals that God had commanded this widow woman to feed Elijah. Jesus said that Elijah had been sent to this specific widow. This was a divine connection and she already had a word from God. Yet, here's this negative confession.

An Act of Faith

Personally, I believe the widow was wavering in her faith a little bit. God had spoken to her and she had a revelation. She was believing Him for supernatural supply, but not strongly enough to speak it. This is exactly the reason why God led Elijah to ask for her last little bit of food. She needed to take a step of faith. She needed to get beyond that doubt and unbelief and step out into the realm of faith.

You'll find this truth also in the ministry of Jesus. The blind man on the side of the road cried out, "Jesus, thou son of David, have mercy on me" (Mark 10:47). Everybody told him to shut up, but it didn't bother him. He just cried out all the louder. Then the Lord asked him what he wanted, and when the blind man requested return of his sight, Jesus answered, "Go thy way; thy faith hath made thee whole" (Mark 10:52).

The blind man had already overcome opposition and had taken a step of faith, so the Lord told him his faith had made him whole. But when others in need of healing were pointed out to Jesus, like the man who was born blind (John 9), He told them to go do something. If you study this out, you will find that the people who didn't take an initial step toward Jesus were given something to do before they could receive their miracle. To those who took steps toward Him, He said things like, "According to your faith be it unto you" (Matthew 9:29). When someone was strong enough in faith, all they had to do was reach out and touch the hem of His garment and healing flowed—without Jesus doing anything! (Mark 5:25-34.) But the Lord had to solicit some response, some act of faith, from other people.

They Need to Give

This widow from Zarephath had a revelation, but she was struggling with it. That's precisely why Elijah asked her to give of her food. If she would have been stronger in faith, it's possible that he may not have made this same demand of her. He was trying to help her.

Ministers need to do the same thing when they receive offerings and encourage people to give. One of the ways Satan has hindered the flow of finances in the body of Christ is through preachers who view the request for tithes and offerings as a plea for finances for themselves. If they see it that way, they're always going to be bashful and apologetic when they call God's people to bring their tithes and offerings. They're going to be timid because they don't want to portray themselves as trying to take from the people. But the truth is, we're asking the people to give for them, not us!

Elijah was the prophet of God. He was blessed. Elijah could have eaten at the best restaurant and stayed in the best hotel in Zarephath. He didn't need this widow's food for himself. This was actually provision for that woman. He was asking her to give the last thing she had to benefit herself, not him.

If you're a minister, you need to change your mindset: *I'm not just giving this offering talk, encouraging the people to sow and receiving this money, for me. I'm doing it for them. They need to give!* If you could just make that change in your thinking, it will make a difference in your finances and in the ability of your people to receive from God.

Encouraged to Step Out

What would happen today if you went into a town, saw a widow, and found out that she only had one last little bit of food? What would happen if she and her son were about to die, and you took her welfare check right out of her hand saying, "Give it to me!" If you took her last little bit of food, the *Sidon Post* would have been all over it! The headline would read, "Prophet Takes Widow's Last Bit!" However, Elijah wasn't doing this for his sake; he was doing it for her sake.

Elijah knew that this was "the" woman. He knew that he had her miracle, but if he didn't become aggressive, she wasn't going to receive it. If she didn't get out of her negative attitude saying, "This is all I have. I'm going to die," she was going to miss God's provision.

Most of us would feel sympathy for that woman, and instead of taking her last little bit of food, we would shell out and give to her. Giving her some food might feed her one more day, but taking from her what she had would give her a supply that would last nearly three years!

Many times our compassion is misdirected. People don't need a hand out; they need a hand up. Elijah was doing what was best for this widow woman. He was saving her life by asking for her last little bit of food.

Give Me All You Have

Once I was ministering on this passage in Decatur, Texas, and a woman came up for prayer at the end of the service and asked me if I remembered her. I told her that I was sorry, but I didn't. She said I had prayed with her a year ago for her release from a mental hospital. She was a patient at the time of our first meeting and had come to church on a Sunday pass. I prayed with her and she was eventually released from the hospital. She was so changed in her appearance that I didn't recognize her.

But now she had another prayer request. Though she wasn't a patient at the mental facility anymore, she was the janitor there and they supplied her with room and board. She wanted a new job and a new place to live.

I had just taught about this widow at Zarepath, so I asked the woman what she had. She went back to her seat, got her purse and counted $83.23. She said this was all the money she had, and she had to make it last for another ten days until she got paid again. I told her to give all she had – all $83.23. Just so people wouldn't think I was doing this just to get all of her money for myself, I gave all her money to the pastor of the local church. Then I prayed for her and believed she was going to receive big time!

The pastor of that church called me the next week. He told me that the day after I received this woman's offering, a man came to her who hadn't been at the church service and didn't know what had happened, and gave her a car. It wasn't brand-new, but it was nice, and that was something she hadn't even asked for. On Wednesday of that week, the woman's mother called to see how she was doing. They had been estranged from each other because of the woman's mental problems. They hadn't talked in over a year. When the mother found out the woman had been released from the mental facility, she repented for the way things had gone and asked her daughter to come back home and live with her.

This woman was not only given someplace else to live besides the mental institution, but she had the relationship with her mother restored. And by Friday of that week, she had a new job paying her twice as much! I imagine someone at that church service was highly offended at me for taking all of this woman's money. There was a time when I also would have been offended if I had seen a minister do that. But I've come to realize that we aren't taking from people when we encourage them to give. We are giving to them, just like Elijah did with this widow in Zarepath.

As a minister, you need to recognize that the greatest thing you can do for people is get their money from them. I know how terrible that sounds, but if you do this with the motive that I'm sharing here, you will actually be helping them. You need to challenge God's people to give, and then receive their offering with the right attitude. That's one of the best things you can do for them!

We ministers, myself included, haven't been bold in the area of finances because we don't want to be perceived as being after people's money. We have let the devil intimidate us. We think that we are receiving the offering for us, when in reality we're receiving it for the people! When I minister on healing, deliverance, or anything else, I'm preaching those messages for the people—not for myself. But when it comes to ministering on finances, we become timid and lose the anointing and power of the message.

Every believer needs to be encouraged to step out in faith. As ministers, it's our responsibility to challenge them. We need to push them to get out there and do what God has called them to do!

Chapter Six

Step Out in Faith!

The Word says that Elijah didn't just tell the widow woman, "Give me your food." He gave her a promise, or a word from God, to go with it. "And Elijah said unto her, Fear not; go and do as thou hast said: but make me thereof a little cake first, and bring it unto me, and after make for thee and for thy son. For thus saith the LORD God of Israel, The barrel of meal shall not waste, neither shall the cruse of oil fail, until the day that the LORD sendeth rain upon the earth" (1 Kings 17:13-14).

Elijah gave the widow the word of God—the same word that he had been living under that had been meeting his need. We shouldn't just ask people for money without giving them something to stand on. We shouldn't encourage people to give without giving them the Word of God to anchor their faith. People shouldn't be giving because of your charisma or need. They should be giving because they've been given God's Word and have been challenged to step out in faith.

God's Best

Elijah challenged this woman's faith and gave her the word of the Lord to stand on, "And she went and did…" (1 Kings 17:15). She obeyed the word of God. Notice how Elijah said, "Make me thereof a little cake **first**…" (1 Kings 17:13; emphasis mine). You need to challenge folks to give God their best. People say, "Well, I want to give. I really desire to give and as soon as God prospers me and I get anything extra, I'm going to give!" In other words, they're giving God what they can afford, what's left over after their needs are taken care of. They aren't putting the Lord and His kingdom first (Matthew 6:33).

I'm not legalistic with this. There have actually been times when someone has come up to me and asked, "My rent is due and I just received a $500 check. Do I give off this first or pay my rent?" The truth is, it depends on where they are. I've told people before, "Pay your rent. It's a miracle!" However, I wouldn't personally do that. It didn't matter how bad our need was, every time Jamie and I received provision, we would give off it first. But I'm not going to condemn someone else for not doing this.

When you give God your best, He begins to give you His best. As long as you are just giving what you can afford after all your bills are paid, you aren't ever going to see God's best.

Daily Bread

Elijah said, "Give to me first." This wasn't just a one-time deal. The widow had to do this every day until the drought ended. The Bible doesn't tell us the exact length of time the drought persisted while she was providing for Elijah, but it was probably around two and a half to three years that this little bit of oil and meal sustained them. She didn't give to Elijah once and get three years' supply of oil and meal. There was always that tiny little bit, but it never failed!

There was never a great supply, but there was always enough. There was never so much that she could just coast and say, "Well, I don't have to believe God today." No! Every morning, she faced this choice—make for the man of God first and believe that there will be enough for her and her son, or not. She had to exercise her faith every day to obey the word of the Lord.

That's a great miracle, but most of us wouldn't like this miracle at all. Jesus taught us to pray, "Give us this day our daily bread" (Matthew 6:11). We don't like *daily* bread. We like to get enough to set two or three years worth aside, so we can feel safe and secure. Yet the Lord said we were to ask for "daily bread."

The widow's miracle had to take place every single day. And every day, she was probably tempted to say, "This is our last little bit. I think I'll make for us first." But she stepped out in faith and made for the man of God first. This is how the Lord met her need. What a tremendous lesson!

You don't have to experience everything on your own. You can learn from the examples recorded in God's Word. You can learn from how God dealt with this woman through Elijah.

Raised from the Dead

This woman's giving not only affected her, but it also affected her son. Later in this passage (1 Kings 17:17-23), we see recorded that the woman's son died. By this time, she had been walking by faith and giving to the man of God first every day for quite some time. She had been giving, therefore she could expect to receive. She had a right to make a demand on him to raise up her son.

This is the first instance in Scripture of anyone being raised from the dead. It hadn't been done prior to this time. There was no precedent for it. Seeing someone raised from the dead today is still unusual.

Once I met a minister from Salt Lake City who had raised eight people from the dead—two of whom were in the same service! I've personally seen several people raised from the dead, including my own son. Even though it's unusual, we have a precedent for it. However, Elijah didn't have Scripture like we do today. There had never been a real miracle ministry before him, other than the miracles Moses performed to get the children of Israel out of Egypt. So there was no precedent for this, nothing to encourage Elijah in his faith. Yet, Elijah went in and raised this woman's son from the dead. This was a result of the faith the woman demonstrated through her giving.

Faithful in the Least

Faithful giving won't just open a door for you in your finances; it will open a door for you in many other areas of your life and ministry. "He that is faithful in that which is least is faithful also in much: and he that is unjust in the least is unjust also in much. If therefore ye have not been faithful in the unrighteous mammon **[money]**, who will commit to your trust the true riches?" (Luke 16:10-11; brackets mine)

Jesus called money the "least" area of stewardship. If you can't trust God in finances, you're not operating in enough faith to really trust Him in healing, deliverance, and other things either. If you can't jump ten feet, then you certainly can't jump thirty. If you can't do the lesser, you certainly can't do the greater. Everyone understands this in the natural realm.

If you can't trust God with your money, how are you ever going to trust Him with your eternal salvation, health, family, church, ministry, or anything else? When you start being faithful in the area of finances, it will open up doors in other areas of your life. Faithfulness in finances is the starting place. For additional insights on this important principle, please refer to my teaching entitled, *The Least of These.*

Destined for Success

Everyone in the body of Christ is at varying stages of growth, ministry, and God working in their lives. However, the Lord's thoughts and plans for each of us are "thoughts of peace, and not of evil, to give you an expected end" (Jeremiah 29:11). God hasn't destined anyone for failure. He never makes a dud, junk, or a mistake. The Lord has destined you for success!

Success with God isn't the same as worldly success. My friend, Lawson Perdue, began his ministry in a town of 250 people, and had 100 of them coming to his church. Some people may think, *Well, that's only 100 people in his church.* But that's 40 percent of the population. If a pastor could get that percentage of the population of Colorado Springs to attend his church, that would be 200,000 people! You need to be careful how you evaluate success. It's not just dependent on numbers, finances, and other such things.

God wills for every one of us to succeed in whatever area He's planted us. He has a perfect plan, but we must also do our part; there are some things we need to go and do. We need to be faithful and take the steps He prescribes. This widow of Zarephath was faithful to do what the man of God told her to do at the word of the Lord. We can't receive God's provision if we won't step out in faith and do what He tells us to do.

Many times we struggle because we aren't "there," because we are not doing what the Lord has called us to do. We have a word from God. It's time we stepped out in faith!

Chapter Seven

Where the Fruit Is

Every year I take a team of our Bible college students with me to minister over in the U.K. Last year, a woman with multiple sclerosis came to the meetings in her wheelchair. She had only been born again for two months, but had been listening to my tapes. She told me, "I came to be healed. I'm getting out of this wheelchair before the week is over!"

During my message, I referred to her and said, "We're agreeing with you and believing." As soon as I finished preaching, the students were down there ministering to this woman. They prayed for her and she got out of that wheelchair. Before the week was over, she was walking up and down the stairs and pushing her wheelchair. She got baptized and healed. It was awesome!

Every day on the bus, the students would share what had happened that day and how God had asked them to do what they felt inadequate to do. Some didn't feel adequate to lead someone to the Lord so they would pray, "Oh God, don't let anyone come up to me in the prayer line who needs salvation. Let me pray for something else!" Others felt inadequate to minister the Baptism in the Holy Spirit or healing.

What they discovered was that whatever they felt inadequate to do, was exactly the thing they had to do every time without exception! If they said, "I don't want to pray for someone to be healed so just let it be a headache, nothing big," then someone blind would come up to them. They would lay hands on them, and their blind eyes would open!

The reason these students saw God do things they had never seen Him do before was because they put themselves in a position where they needed the Lord to do something supernatural. The truth is that most of us never stretch ourselves out in faith. Therefore, we don't need God to do anything. Most of us don't ever go out and lay hands on somebody because we're afraid it won't work. Guess what? You're right! If you don't lay hands on a person, they won't ever be healed!

However, if you do put yourself in a position where you're standing up front and you're the one who is supposed to be ministering, people will come and make a demand on you. If you just close your eyes, before you know it, God will do a miracle in spite of you. Most of us have never allowed ourselves to be in a position where we need a supernatural manifestation of the power of God. We play it too safe.

The fruit is out on the limb, but we're all hugging the trunk. We need to get out on the limb and bob up and down in the breeze a little bit. Get out there where it feels a little insecure.

That's where the fruit is—out on a limb! You must take a step of faith. Until you get to where you're doing something beyond your ability, there's no reason for God to show up. There's no reason for a miracle.

God will always cause you to do the thing that seems impossible. If it's possible, it's not God. The Lord will lead you to do something strange, uncomfortable, and different. He will tell you to take a widow woman's last little bit of food, knowing that in the natural, that food is the only way she'll ever make it. Most of us would rather do it some other way, but God's way leads us to prosper (Luke 6:38).

My Last Quarter

When I first started ministering in Segoville, Texas, a guy came through town asking for a handout. He needed something to eat and a place to sleep. It was pitiful. This fellow had left his wife and kids back in Michigan while he came down to Texas to look for work. He had been there two months, spent all his money, and was facing foreclosure on his home. He was down to a quarter, which he was saving to call his wife if something came up. I could tell this guy was a hard worker, but he was discouraged and was having trouble finding a job.

He came by our church while my friend and I were there. I was preparing to shell out the money for a motel room and something to eat, when my friend asked him, "How much do you have?"

The man replied, "I have one quarter left so I can make a phone call."

"Give it to me," my friend said. "We're going to agree with you and pray and believe God for a miracle."

When my friend did that, I became really embarrassed, thinking, *He's going to take this guy's last little bit of money!* I felt so bad about it, because my friend didn't give the man anything. This guy slept outside that night on the street. We didn't give him any food, but we took his quarter as an offering. That didn't satisfy me. I felt terrible and struggled with this all night long.

However, first thing in the morning, this guy was knocking on our door. A fellow from one of the places where he had put in a job application a month or two earlier, came up to him on the street that night and exclaimed, "I've finally found you! I'm going to make you the foreman of my ranch. You'll have good pay and a three-bedroom home. I'll even send for your family and bring them here." By the end of the morning, this guy had a job, a new home, a big salary, and his family on the way. Praise God!

I would have given the man a meal and one night's lodging, thinking I was doing something awesome for him. But my friend took this guy's last quarter and gave him a brand new job, a place to live, and brought his family together. God is awesome!

Godly Confidence

We have a word from God, but we've been timid and shy about it. None of these things we see in the life of Elijah would have happened if he had been bashful with what God had spoken to him. He went right to the top—to the king—and declared, "According to my word...." Most of us would immediately say, "Well, you arrogant thing!" But you need to have that kind of attitude—not arrogance, but confidence – because of what God has done in your life.

There's a fine line between godly confidence and arrogance. However, the greatest step of humility is to actually stand up and declare, "I'm your answer. I'm the one. I have a word from God for you!" It takes a lot of humility to say something like that. It takes a lot of humility to really declare what the Lord has put in your heart and get beyond the fear of man and thinking, *What will they think of me? What are they going to say?*

God has probably spoken some things to you that you haven't seen manifest yet, so you're afraid to speak it. You're afraid to act on it. You're afraid to do the things that God has put in your heart because of what other people will say. If Elijah had been like that, none of these things would have ever taken place.

Some people could misuse what I'm sharing, but I believe that you are someone who is seeking first God's kingdom. You don't minister to others for selfish reasons or to promote yourself. You genuinely love God and want to see other people blessed. Therefore, it's time you recognized that you have a word from God. That word is what gives you authority and power, not the recognition of people, your theological training, etc.

Elijah didn't come and introduce himself. He didn't tell who he was or show the miracles he had done before to give verification and authority to what he said. He just spoke the word of God. That's what we're all called to do. God is the one who confirms the Word. He's the One who brings it to pass. Our responsibility is to speak it forth in faith. Many of us just haven't been bold in speaking the Word. We need to believe the word that God has given us!

Preach Your Word

While in Kansas City, I went over to someone's house for a meal. There may have been a dozen people sitting at the table, but this one woman never said a word. Throughout the entire time, I tried to be polite and engage her in conversation but she wouldn't talk. She just sat there. So finally, I singled her out in front of everyone and asked, "Who are you?"

This woman was on a mission from God! She turned toward me, stated her name, and said, "A year ago I was in a mental institution, condemned to be there for life. I was totally out of my mind and had lost it. Then someone gave me your message entitled *Grace and Faith*. I listened to that tape at least a hundred times, and it's totally revolutionized my life. I'm transformed, and I'm completely free today!"

Then she got right up in my face and declared, "You have a revelation of grace that would set every person in a mental institution free if they could hear it. You need to be preaching grace!" She just jumped all over my case! God spoke to me through her. All of a sudden, I realized that I hadn't fully esteemed and valued what God had given me to the degree that I should have. Although I had been preaching grace, I saw that this woman believed the word I was preaching even more than I did—and I got convicted!

Sometimes, you need to go back and reevaluate things. God has done some awesome things in your life. He's changed you from the inside out. You need to believe the Word of God and do something with it. You have a message that would change millions of people. Appreciate what you have. Don't let the devil talk you out of it. Stand on, act on, and confidently proclaim the Word of God in your heart. Go out on the limb; that's where the fruit is!

Chapter Eight

Listen to God

"And it came to pass after many days, that the word of the LORD came to Elijah in the third year, saying, Go, shew thyself unto Ahab; and I will send rain upon the earth" (1 Kings 18:1). The drought began when Elijah heard the voice of God. The Lord said to tell King Ahab there would be a drought (1 Kings 17:1). Elijah heard the word of the Lord to go to the Brook Cherith (1 Kings 17:2-4). Then God told him to go to a widow in Zarephath (1 Kings 17:8-9). The entire chain of events hinges on Elijah hearing and obeying God's voice.

Elijah didn't do anything for three years until the word of the Lord came to him. It's amazing how impatient we become when we don't hear anything new from God. Many times, we just go out and do things on our own. Like Abraham, we create Ishmaels (Genesis 16). The Lord might have given us a promise, but it doesn't seem like it's coming to pass so we try to help Him out in the flesh. Elijah didn't do that. He chose to stay in tune with God. He lived his life at the word of the Lord.

Pay Attention

Jesus said, "My sheep hear my voice, and I know them, and they follow me…And a stranger will they not follow, but will flee from him: for they know not the voice of strangers" (John 10:27, 5). This, however, is not the experience of many Christians. In fact, it's exactly the opposite. Many Christians complain about not being able to hear the voice of God, but then they'll turn around in the next breath and say, "The devil told me I'm never going to hear God's voice. Satan says this and Satan says that." They hear the devil with no problem at all, but they have trouble hearing God. Yet the Word says, "My sheep hear My voice and a stranger they will not follow!" We are simply living below our privileges. We need to tune in and start listening to God's voice!

"Howbeit when he, the Spirit of truth, is come, he will guide you into all truth: for he shall not speak of himself; but whatsoever he shall hear, that shall he speak: and he will show you things to come" (John 16:13). While reading this verse several years ago, I started wondering what it would be like if the Lord actually showed us things to come. How would knowing what was going to happen impact your wisdom, your financial investments and others things like that? As I meditated on this, I determined to start focusing to listen for a word from God. Most of the time we don't hear what God is saying to us because we aren't inclining our ears and paying attention.

Things to Come

I began listening for the Lord to speak to me of things to come. At the time, we had our horses in a little mountain community called Green Mountain Falls. A friend of ours allowed me to keep my horses on his property, free of charge. He loved having them there. Every time we saw him, he would say, "It's so wonderful having your horses. I don't have to mow anymore. They're great!"

Then the Lord spoke to me and said, "You're going to lose that place for your horses soon. You need to find another one." At first I thought, *This is weird! This guy loves having our horses there. He thanks me every time I see him.* But I recognized the voice of the Lord, so after a week or so, I started looking for another place to house our horses. I didn't have any reason to do so other than the prompting of God in my heart. I was actually going to have to pay some money to house them at another place, whereas this guy was letting me use his pasture for free.

I found another place for my horses and planned to move them on Wednesday. I hadn't said anything about this to my friend, but he came up to me on Sunday and declared, "I can't stand it one minute longer! Those horses have to be off my property by Tuesday!" This was the first time he had ever given me any indication that he wasn't pleased with our arrangement. That was Sunday, and by Tuesday they had to be gone.

I thought, *God was really speaking to me. He told me of things to come!* So instead of being upset or surprised, I was actually blessed. The Holy Spirit had shown me things to come. So I started praying about some other things, and doing so opened up a number of doors for the ministry. We don't draw on the word of the Lord enough! It's available, but we have to appropriate it.

Elijah didn't do anything until he heard a word from God. Many of the problems we encounter today are totally self-created. We blame the devil saying, "Satan did this and that." Of course, the enemy takes advantage of everything we give him. He may be the one taking shots at us, but we're the ones giving him all the ammunition. You can save yourself a lot of problems by just getting to the place where you hear the voice of the Lord.

"Show Yourself to Ahab"

So here Elijah was, three years after the start of the drought. He didn't do anything until the word of the Lord came to him and said, "Go show yourself to Ahab." But once he heard from God, that's exactly what he did. "And Elijah went to show himself unto Ahab. And there was a sore famine in Samaria. And Ahab called Obadiah, which was the governor of his house. (Now Obadiah feared the LORD greatly: For it was so, when Jezebel cut off the prophets of the LORD, that Obadiah took an hundred prophets, and hid them by fifty in a cave, and fed them with bread and water.) And Ahab said unto Obadiah, Go into the land, unto all fountains of water, and unto all brooks: peradventure we may find grass to save the horses and mules alive, that we lose not all the beasts" (1 Kings 18:2-5). This famine was so severe, that it looked like they were going to start losing their livestock. "So they divided the land between them to pass throughout it: Ahab went one way by himself, and Obadiah went another way by himself. And as Obadiah was in the way, behold, Elijah met him: and he knew him, and fell on his face, and said, Art thou that my lord Elijah? And he answered him, I am: go, tell thy lord, Behold, Elijah is here" (1 Kings 18:6-8).

"I'm the Only One"

"And he said, What have I sinned, that thou wouldest deliver thy servant into the hand of Ahab, to slay me? As the LORD thy God liveth, there is no nation or kingdom, whither my lord hath not sent to seek thee: and when they said, He is not there; he took an oath of the kingdom and nation, that they found thee not. And now thou sayest, Go, tell thy lord, Behold, Elijah is here. And it shall come to pass, as soon as I am gone from thee, that the spirit of the LORD shall carry thee whither I know not; and so when I come and tell Ahab, and he cannot find thee, he shall slay me: but I thy servant fear the LORD from my youth. Was it not told my lord what I did when Jezebel slew the prophets of the LORD, how I hid an hundred men of the LORD's prophets by fifty in a cave, and fed them with bread and water?" (1 Kings 18:9-13).

Notice what Obadiah told Elijah. Obadiah told him right here that he had hid and fed a hundred of the Lord's ministers.

Most people think Elijah was sincere when he said a few days later, "But Lord, I'm the only one left!" (1 Kings 19:10). But Elijah wasn't being sincere. He knew there were other prophets still alive. This will be an important factor later. Let's look at that passage again: "And now thou sayest, Go, tell thy lord, Behold, Elijah is here: and he shall slay me. And Elijah said, As the LORD of hosts liveth, before whom I stand, I will surely shew myself unto him today. So Obadiah went to meet Ahab, and told him: and Ahab went to meet Elijah" (1 Kings 18:14-16).

Satan Tries to Intimidate

Notice what Ahab had to say to Elijah when they saw each other face to face: "And it came to pass, when Ahab saw Elijah, that Ahab said unto him, Art thou he that troubleth Israel?" (1 Kings 18:17) Now notice Elijah's response to Ahab's accusation: "And he answered, I have not troubled Israel; but thou, and thy father's house, in that ye have forsaken the commandments of the LORD, and thou hast followed Baalim" (1 Kings 18:18).

Elijah had a word from God. He came back to tell Ahab that the Lord was going to send rain, and the very first thing Ahab said was, "Are you the one who's troubling Israel?" He tried to make Elijah feel responsible for all of the problems Israel was facing.

Satan is an intimidator. He's an accuser who, sooner or later, will twist things around in an attempt to make you feel like you're the problem. He will bring thoughts like, *These people would have been better off if you had never been here.* He'll try to tell you all kinds of things. We see this big time in our society today.

In the last days, people will call evil "good," and good "evil" (Isaiah 5:20). When you stand up today and say that homosexuality is wrong—without being mad at anyone or condemning anyone, and being motivated by a genuine desire to see people set free by the truth (John 8:32)—people will turn what you've said to make you out to be the "bigot," the one who's "prejudiced" and "closed-minded."

Have you ever noticed that the only people who can be openly criticized in our society today are Christians? We're the only ones whose case it's politically correct to get on. You can't criticize any other group. You can't run the risk of offending anyone. However, you can call Christians anything you want.

It's amazing how the devil has turned this thing around. Because of his intimidation, most Christians are afraid to speak the truth. We're afraid to act on the word God has given us.

This was exactly what Ahab was trying to do to the prophet. But Elijah answered, "I haven't troubled Israel. It's you and your house who have brought all this upon yourselves!"

Refuse to Receive It

The same thing happened with Jesus. When He came down off the Mount of Transfiguration, they brought a demonized boy to Him. The father said, "If you can do anything, please have mercy on us" (Mark 9:22, my paraphrase). The way he said it basically put the ball entirely in Jesus' court. But Jesus wouldn't accept this, and neither should we. Jesus immediately turned around and said. "If thou canst believe, all things are possible to him that believeth" (Mark 9:23).

The Lord wasn't going to accept responsibility that wasn't His. He knew this boy's father could believe God, so He turned the responsibility back onto him saying, "It's you. You have to believe! If you can believe, this will happen."

The devil will constantly try to put all of the burden and responsibility on you. Elijah just refused to receive it. He boldly declared, "It's not my fault all this happened—it's yours! You're the one who brought this whole thing on yourself." He wasn't about to be intimidated by the devil, and neither should you!

Chapter Nine

Boldly Speak His Word

"**N**ow therefore send, and gather to me all Israel unto mount Carmel, and the prophets of Baal four hundred and fifty, and the prophets of the groves four hundred, which eat at Jezebel's table. So Ahab sent unto all the children of Israel, and gathered the prophets together unto mount Carmel" (1 Kings 18:19-20). Elijah just showed up on the scene and the word of God put him in control. At first, nobody knew who he was. The Bible doesn't record how Ahab initially responded to Elijah. But since Elijah was bold enough to speak the word the Lord had given him, even when nothing at the time was happening; his words gained credibility in the eyes of others when things came to pass.

Some people really got into that Y2K computer thing. They were literally prophesying the beginning of tribulation and the end of civilization as we know it. I sent a letter in the fall of 1999 to my mailing list stating, "Prophecy is not my thing, but I don't believe all this Y2K stuff is credible." Then I listed my points and said, "Remember *88 Reasons Why Jesus is Going to Return in '88*, the

Jupiter Effect, and all those other things? None of them came to anything. Neither will Y2K!"

People are always "prophesying" doom and gloom, but I just don't buy into it so I decided to stick my neck out and go on record before Y2K arrived. Although I received some criticism, most of the initial response was positive. However, after Y2K passed and nothing happened, I gained a lot of credibility with many people who had previously written me off.

That's exactly what Elijah did right here. Due to his boldness to proclaim the word of God, the king had sought him in every nation on the face of the earth (1 Kings 18:10).

If you stick around long enough, you'll see the word of God put you in a position of authority every single time. However, you must be truly speaking God's Word, not just your own doctrines and opinions. Sooner or later, the word of God will always exalt you.

Mix with Faith

God doesn't actually exalt ministers. He exalts His Word. It's the Word of God He's after. That's what will truly change people. We put so much emphasis on our actions and charisma but if you look at the people God has used throughout history, many of them had nothing going for them. All they had was the word of the Lord and genuine faith in it.

Speaking specifically of the Jews who had rejected the Gospel, Hebrews 4:2 says: "The word preached did not profit them, not being mixed with faith in them that heard it." You need to mix the Word you've heard with faith. Then, once you really believe the word He's given you, it will put you over. Speak the word God has put in your mouth and it will give you authority in the lives of people.

Jonathan Edwards sparked the Great Awakening in the United States. An extreme introvert, this guy also could barely see. He wore big old Coke-bottle type glasses. Edwards wrote out his messages in large letters. To deliver them, all he would do was stand up, hold the paper in front of his face, read the message, and every once in awhile, point. That's all he did! Because of the faith he had in the word God had given him to preach, Edwards spoke with power and authority, and basically led the struggling colonies to a great revival.

Prophets Speak to Kings

"If any man speak, let him speak as the oracles of God" (1 Peter 4:11). Elijah was bold! He confidently spoke the word the Lord had given him. Elijah told Ahab, "Call all the prophets of Baal and the groves together. Assemble the whole nation. Meet me at Mount Carmel!" And the king, bowing to the man of God, answered, "Yes, sir. Right away!"

The word of the Lord in Elijah's mouth had been proven. It came to pass. The king saw the power of the word of God.

Therefore, it put Elijah in the driver's seat. A prophet told the king what to do—and he did it. That's the way it ought to be!

The officials in your town ought to go to the leaders of the body of Christ there and ask, "What would you like done?" We're the ones with the word of God. There was a time in the United States when it was like that. You couldn't schedule a sports event on a Sunday, a Wednesday night, or at any other "church time." Why? Because the church was an authority in people's lives.

The breakdown started in the pulpit. We became apologetic and substituted other things for God and His Word. We need to be authoritative with the Word of God. I'm not talking about authority and boldness in yourself, but about believing the word God has given you.

We ought to be going up to some government officials and saying, "What you're doing is wrong. This is wrong. Change! Repent!" You don't have to condemn them. You say these things in love, but be bold and speak the Word of God. It's not the Word that's changed; it's the people who represent the Word who have changed!

Make a Decision

"And Elijah came unto all the people, and said, How long halt ye between two opinions? if the LORD be God, follow him: but if Baal, then follow him. And the people answered him not a word" (1 Kings 18:21). A minister is supposed to challenge people to make a decision. But many times we're afraid to do this because they might make a wrong choice and it could work against us. People may leave, but you must bring them to a place of commitment. When Elijah called the people to make a commitment, the people didn't answer him one word.

You Cut Yourself Off

"Then said Elijah unto the people, I, even I only, remain a prophet of the LORD; but Baal's prophets are four hundred and fifty men" (1 Kings 18:22). Elijah knew better than that. Remember, he had just been told that there were still a hundred prophets being hid in caves by Obadiah (1 Kings 18:13). Although what Elijah said was incorrect, it should encourage you and me. God used Elijah to call down fire from heaven, even while he was in deception, arrogance, and pride. He thought he was the only one left serving God, but the Lord still used him.

You don't have to be perfect for God to use you. Elijah had a word from God, was faithful to that word, and acted on it—but he had some problems. This doesn't mean that it's okay to have problems. These same issues caused Elijah to crash and burn in 1 Kings 19. Elijah really cut short his ministry. He didn't even fulfill a third of what God wanted him to do. The Lord had much more for Elijah than what he accomplished.

Even though these wrong attitudes and mistakes in our lives are deadly and we need to deal with them, the Lord will still use us. It's not God who rejects us. We destroy ourselves. "They that observe lying vanities forsake their own mercy" (Jonah 2:8). We cut ourselves off—not God. When we observe lying vanities, we open ourselves up to the devil.

Doctrine or Proof?

"Let them therefore give us two bullocks; and let them choose one bullock for themselves, and cut it in pieces, and lay it on wood, and put no fire under: and I will dress the other bullock, and lay it on wood, and put no fire under: and call ye on the name of your gods, and I will call on the name of the LORD: and the God that answereth by fire, let him be God. And all the people answered and said, It is well spoken" (1 Kings 18:23-24). Elijah called for a test saying, "Let's see who the real God is!" This is so simple. We're the ones who have the power, reality, and anointing of the Lord. We're the ones who can lay hands on the sick and they will recover. However, most ministers are preaching words without manifesting the supernatural evidence of God with signs and wonders following.

If we would just operate in the full Gospel with supernatural attestation to God's Word, laying hands on and seeing people raised from the dead, it would stop a lot of mouths. We would silence many people if we just started demonstrating things. I've actually done this before. I've told people, "Alright! You say your god is true. I say my God is true. Let's try it! Let's see who can do what!" We just put them to a test. It works! Those people don't have any power.

I remember when a Jehovah's Witness came to our door and was spilling all of his doctrine on me. I told him, "I know that God is real. I know the God I'm serving is the true God."

He asked, "How can you know that?"

I just started pointing around the room and saying, "See this? It was a miracle!" I pointed to everything we had. It was a miracle that God provided. Then I told him about the dead being raised and blind eyes being opened—things that I've personally seen. That's when he hit the door running! The Jehovah's Witnesses have a doctrine, but they don't have an experience. They don't have any proof or reality to what they're saying.

Put Up or Shut Up

We're playing it too safe. We need to be bold. God doesn't mind being put on the spot. A minister friend of mine says, "The more boldly I talk about what God is going to do, the bigger He shows up!" God is bigger than we have ever thought about, yet we're afraid we're going to say something or promise something that He can't deliver. That's not true! God is more than able to deliver.

When we are bold, we're not really putting the Lord on the spot. We're putting ourselves on the spot. God is willing and able. He's more than capable. It's me I'm putting out there when I say, "God is going to do this and that." We need to stretch ourselves. We need to believe God for some supernatural miracles.

I remember one service I was in where the people just weren't receptive to what I was sharing. It was obvious from the beginning that it wasn't a good situation. Do you know what I did? Two or three minutes into the service, I just said, "Let's have show and tell. We're going to demonstrate and then I'll explain it to you. The first person who stands up here is going to be healed."

People came forward, I prayed for them, and God healed them and set them free. You get people's attention after something like that. We can do this! You might say, "But Andrew, I don't have the gift of healing." Neither do I! I don't have the gift of miracles either, but I've seen blind eyes and deaf ears opened. I've seen the dead raised!

When I pray for people, I am doing nothing but operating as a believer. I don't have a supernatural "anointing" or ministry gift for healing. I just pray a prayer of faith based on God's Word, and I see miracles happen all the time. Every believer can do this. The Bible says that God confirms His Word with signs and wonders following (Mark 16:20). If you're truly sharing the Word, there should be signs and wonders following.

In a sense, Elijah was saying, "Alright—put up or shut up! You have a doctrine. I have a doctrine. Let's see which one has any power in it."

"Not in Word, but Power"

Paul wrote the same thing to the Corinthians. Some were saying, "I'm of Paul," others were claiming "I'm of Cephas," and still others "I'm of Apollos" (1 Corinthians 1:12). Finally, Paul declared: "But I will come to you shortly, if the Lord will, and will know, not the speech of them which are puffed up, but the power. For the kingdom of God is not in word, but in power" (1 Corinthians 4:19-20).

Basically, Paul was saying, "We're going to solve this problem when I come. Those of you who have any power operating in your lives can talk. But if you haven't healed any sick, cleansed any lepers, ministered sight to the blind, or raised someone from the dead in the last month or two—then you have to sit down and shut up!"

One time, my friend and I went to Roswell, New Mexico, and ministered in a Baptist church. This was back when I was still Baptist. It was the first meeting we'd ever held. We got in trouble for what we were sharing in the church, so they invited us over to the Baptist Student Union building instead. After we stood up and gave our testimonies, they started yelling at us saying, "God doesn't do miracles like that today! Besides, the children of Israel crossed the 'Reed' Sea, not the Red Sea." My friend answered, "Well, if all those Egyptians and horses drowned in six inches of water, then that's an even greater miracle than I thought!"

Anyway, this "meeting" degenerated fast. They were yelling at us—spouting all kinds of arguments and unbelief. Finally, my friend stood up and declared, "Alright! If your way of doing things is any better than ours, prove it. Those of you who have led someone to the Lord this week can make a statement or ask another question. But if you haven't led anyone to the Lord, then shut up!" Then there was silence. Out of 150 people, nobody was able to say anything. So we just walked right out through the midst of them.

Set the Tone

We need to be more aggressive in our faith. We're so afraid of offending someone. Elijah wouldn't have been viewed as "politically correct." In fact, if Elijah came to your church, most folks would criticize and reject him. He was abrasive, saying, "Let's see who the real God is. Let's put God to a test!" "And call ye on the name of your gods, and I will call on the name of the LORD: and the God that answereth by fire, let him be God. And all the people answered and said, It is well spoken" (1 Kings 18:24).

The people today are ready for this. It's the preachers who aren't. We're the ones playing it safe. Why? We're afraid to preach it because then we'll have to manifest it. If we don't, it'll look like we're just saying words. We're the ones living in fear. Preachers are the ones who set the tone for their church.

As a minister, if you don't like what's happening in your church, you're probably the one who made it that way. I know this isn't always the case; Satan can hinder and you can go through dry spells. But as a whole, you are the one who sets the tone in your ministry. If you aren't seeing the miraculous power of God, then you don't have to look any further than your mirror.

Chapter Ten

Holy Fire

"And Elijah said unto the prophets of Baal, Choose you one bullock for yourselves, and dress it first; for ye are many; and call on the name of your gods, but put no fire under. And they took the bullock which was given them, and they dressed it, and called on the name of Baal from morning even until noon, saying, O Baal, hear us. But there was no voice, nor any that answered. And they leaped upon the altar which was made. And it came to pass at noon, that Elijah mocked them, and said, Cry aloud: for he is a god; either he is talking, or he is pursuing, or he is in a journey, or peradventure he sleepeth, and must be awaked" (1 Kings 18:25-27). Elijah mocked these people. That wasn't very "politically correct." We don't want to offend anyone today. We don't want to say anything about any other group or religion because we're so afraid of offending people. Elijah made fun of them saying, "Maybe you need to yell louder. Either Baal can't hear you or he's asleep!" This is awesome! Elijah knew the power of God.

Doubting God's Willingness

However, for most of us, the issue isn't that we aren't confident of God's power. We don't really doubt that He *can*; we doubt that He *will*. We don't doubt His ability; we doubt His willingness to exercise that ability. Why? Because we know that we aren't everything that we should be.

Elijah's example should be an encouragement to us. He had just told a lie saying, "I'm the only prophet of God left." Yet he was still up there, proclaiming God's power, and the Lord backed him up because he was speaking His word. You don't have to be perfect for God to use you. We let the devil talk us out of our miracle—not because we doubt that God has the power, but because we doubt His willingness to use it on our behalf. We know we don't deserve it.

When Peter walked on the water, he didn't doubt that Jesus could walk on water. When he began to sink, he called out to the Lord for help. Peter didn't doubt Jesus, but when he saw the wind and the waves he started thinking, *What am I doing out here?* Peter doubted that *he* could walk on the water (Matthew 14:28-31). Really, we doubt ourselves because we don't understand the grace and mercy of God. We think we must be perfect before the Lord can use us. Elijah wasn't perfect; he made many mistakes. However, he was so confident and bold that he mocked those false prophets. That's a good attitude!

Nothing Happened

"And they cried aloud, and cut themselves after their manner with knives and lancets, till the blood gushed out and upon them" (1 Kings 18:28). Do you know what they were doing by leaping on the altar and cutting themselves? They were offering their works as a sacrifice. By their actions, they were saying, "Send fire now and we'll be part of the sacrifice!"

This same attitude operates in many Christians today. They think God will use them because of their great sacrifice or because of the things they do. However, it's only by the grace of God that we are used to His glory. We need to extract ourselves out of these things.

Don't make it personal, saying, "Such and such is going to happen because I'm a man (or woman) of God, and this will prove it to you." Instead, we need to constantly remind the people, "This is happening because God is Almighty!" Put all the pressure and responsibility on Him—He can handle it!

That's not what these priests and prophets of Baal were doing by yelling, leaping, and cutting themselves. They thought that somehow their works would cause Baal to answer. And of course, nothing happened. "And it came to pass, when midday was past, and they prophesied until the time of the offering of the evening sacrifice, that there was neither voice, nor any to answer, nor any that regarded" (1 Kings 18:29).

Take Your Best Shot

"And Elijah said unto all the people, Come near unto me. And all the people came near unto him. And he repaired the altar of the LORD that was broken down. And Elijah took twelve stones, according to the number of the tribes of the sons of Jacob, unto whom the word of the LORD came, saying, Israel shall be thy name: And with the stones he built an altar in the name of the LORD: and he made a trench about the altar, as great as would contain two measures of seed. And he put the wood in order, and cut the bullock in pieces, and laid him on the wood and said, Fill four barrels with water, and pour it on the burnt sacrifice, and on the wood. And he said, Do it the second time. And they did it the second time. And he said, Do it the third time. And they did it the third time. And the water ran round about the altar; and he filled the trench also with water" (1 Kings18:30-35).

This whole test Elijah set up was supernatural. There was a bullock and wood, but no fire. However, just so nobody misunderstood and claimed "spontaneous combustion," Elijah had all this water poured over the sacrifice and the altar. Although it was hot and dry because of the drought, only God would be able to set fire to this sacrifice.

Most of us wouldn't do something like that. We would struggle with our own unbelief. We certainly wouldn't do anything to make it harder on ourselves. But Elijah believed God.

Elijah believed he had a word from God. His attitude was, *Devil, take your best shot! Do whatever, but it's going to work!*

What has God called you to do? Is there opposition to you and your word from the Lord? Don't be afraid. Any man or woman with a word from God is bigger than all of his or her opposition. You need to be like Elijah and make it so that only God can bring you through.

If you have faith in the word of God, nothing will shake you. You can actually get to a place where you can say, "Go ahead, devil. Do your worst. I'll still come out smelling like a rose!" Instead of griping and complaining, just rest in the Lord. God has given you a word, so run with it.

If the Lord has called you to do what you're doing, then it will work. Just stay committed and believing. The only thing that can stop you is your unbelief. Elijah was confident. He had faith. He poured water on the wood.

"At Thy Word"

"And it came to pass at the time of the offering of the evening sacrifice, that Elijah the prophet came near, and said, LORD God of Abraham, Isaac, and of Israel, let it be known this day that thou art God in Israel, and that I am thy servant, and that I have done all these things **at thy word**" (1 Kings 18:36; emphasis mine). Elijah knew the drought was going to last years. He said so in 1 Kings 17:1: "There shall not be dew nor rain **these years**, but according to my word" (emphasis mine). During this drought, Elijah must have asked the Lord and meditated on how it would end. Perhaps God had shown him this showdown in a vision. Maybe this was just what Elijah had in his heart. But somehow or another, Elijah had already seen all these things come to pass. That's what he was praying here in 1 Kings 18:36. He said, "I've done all these things at Your word." God had planted all these things inside Elijah and instructed him in it.

If you can't see it on the inside, you'll never see it on the outside. If you can't see your ministry prospering, if you can't see yourself raising someone from the dead, if you can't see blind eyes or deaf ears opening, if you don't meditate on the Word until it becomes a real word to you that you have deep down on the inside, then you cannot have it on the outside.

I have seen many people stumble through ministry who had a word from God. They had a call, but they never sat down and just let that word paint a picture on the inside of them. You must do that! You can't function in faith without doing that.

Paint a Picture

Although I'm not a builder, I occasionally do projects around my house. But before I get started, I have to sit down and really think about what I intend to do. I have to look at the barren ground until I can see the foundation and the support. Then, once I see it on the inside, I can do it on the outside. That's what blueprints are for—to help you see it first on the inside.

Elijah had already seen these things happen. He saw himself challenging the prophets of Baal and knew what the outcome would be. He could see it! Before I ever saw the first person raised from the dead, I took the Word of God that promised this was possible and meditated on it until I could see it in my heart. I saw people raised from the dead on the inside, before I ever saw it on the outside. I saw blind eyes and deaf ears opened on the inside, before I ever saw it happen on the outside.

You need to take God's Word and let it paint a picture. You need to get to where you can see it! Elijah had already seen these things in his heart, so he said, "I'm doing all these things at thy word" (1 Kings 18:36).

The Fire Fell

"Hear me, O LORD, hear me, that this people may know that thou art the LORD God, and that thou hast turned their heart back again. Then the fire of the LORD fell, and consumed the burnt sacrifice, and the wood, and the stones, and the dust, and licked up the water that was in the trench" (1 Kings 18:37-38). This must have been awesome! I've visited this place on Mount Carmel and tried to imagine what it would have been like. This was a mighty miracle of God. Nobody prior to this had ever called down fire from heaven. Solomon had seen the fire of God fall and consume a sacrifice, but he didn't call it down. This was the very first time something like this had ever occurred. And it all happened because the word of the Lord came to Elijah, and he meditated on it, spoke it boldly, and acted on it in obedience. That's awesome!

The same thing can happen with us. Everybody would like to have the results Elijah had, but not everybody wants to do what Elijah did. Not everybody wants to stand up and speak the Word first, and then see the miracles follow. They want to see the miracles first, and then stand up and say, "I was praying and believing for that!"

You need to hear a word from God, get bold with it, and speak it. You'll go through some hard times. Anytime God does something supernatural in your life, there will be a dry, barren spell. Elijah went through the drought and suffered like everybody else. It took faith to get up every day and see that provision, but he believed God—and the fire fell!

Chapter Eleven
Power & Demonstration

The fire of God doesn't just fall anywhere. Elijah had to repair the altar before the fire fell (1 Kings 18:30). Everybody wants the fire of God in their lives, but do they have an altar? Do they have a place where they meet with God? Do they have a personal relationship? Do they spend time alone with the Lord?

People love a fire and will go to great lengths to follow it. If we catch on fire, the world will come watch us burn! If we repair our altar and spend time in the presence of the Consuming Fire himself (Hebrews 12:29), our lives will be set ablaze with His glory and power. "And when all the people saw it, they fell on their faces: and they said, The LORD, he is the God; the LORD, he is the God" (1 Kings 18:39).

This is the first revival recorded in Scripture. It's the first time there was a nationwide move of God. The entire nation fell on their face, saying, "The Lord, He is God! The Lord, He alone is God!" Elijah turned the entire nation back to God through one awesome miracle!

Demonstrate What You Preach

We cannot be effective ministers of God if we minister in word only. There must be some power and demonstration to go with it. T.L. Osborn probably saw more miracles, healings, and salvations in more countries all over the world than anyone else in history. However, he and Daisy began their missionary career trying to minister Christ in word only. After almost a year in India, they returned to the United States confused and disappointed, having been unable to persuade the Muslims and Hindus that they came in contact with that the Bible reveals the true Word of God.

T.L. asked himself the question, "Why would these people believe my Bible more than their 'holy books?' What shows Christianity to be true?" Through a series of profound, life-changing events, the Lord told him, "You must demonstrate the Word you preach!" That's when T.L. began praying for the sick and seeing things happen. Millions were saved and healed by the power of God's Word, boldly proclaimed and demonstrated.

No Compromise

If you see a few people raised from the dead, you'll pack your church out! If you start manifesting miracles in and through your life, they'll start letting people in through the roof. We still have that power; we just aren't using it. Even though the Word we have is superior to what Elijah had (2 Peter 1:19), we don't have the same faith and confidence in it that he did. Yet look what he accomplished. "And Elijah said unto them, Take the prophets of Baal; let not one of them escape. And they took them: and Elijah brought them down to the brook Kishon, and slew them there" (1 Kings 18:40). Elijah killed 450 prophets of Baal and 400 prophets of the groves (1 Kings 18:19). That's awesome!

You may say, "Come on Andrew, I can't relate to that!" I agree that as New Testament believers, God doesn't want us to go out and kill all the people who aren't preaching the truth. However, we do need to get so adamant that we pursue and eradicate all the devil's inroads into our lives. Don't compromise with doubt, unbelief, or failure. Fight until you destroy it! Kill it! Overcome it! We need to have this same militant attitude—not against people, but against the devil. We should hate everything Satan is doing and refuse to take "no" for an answer.

Truth in Tension

Every truth of God must be held in tension. It's like a high wire. A high wire has to be anchored on both sides, or a tight-rope walker won't be able to walk on it. The rope must be firmly anchored and stretched between two opposite points in order to support any weight. Every truth in God's Word has an apparent opposite. Therefore, as much as we believe in God's love, we must also hate the devil. Romans 12:9 says, "Abhor that which is evil; cleave to that which is good." These are apparent opposites. However, you can't just cleave to that which is good and ignore evil. You must hate that which is evil. You have to love the good AND hate the evil, love God AND hate the devil.

Evict the Squatter

"Let not the sun go down upon your wrath: Neither give place to the devil" (Ephesians 4:26-27). Most people interpret this as "Don't go to bed angry. Get it worked out before going to sleep." Although it's beneficial to do that, that's not what this verse is talking about. This verse is saying that you're supposed to have anger for the devil. Don't ever let your anger for the devil go to sleep! Keep it awake!

If you start dozing off and getting complacent, stir yourself up and get angry at the devil. Don't put up with his stuff. If you aren't angry—with a godly anger—you'll give place to the devil. The Lord gave you a capacity for anger, but it's not meant to be used toward other people. It's meant to be used toward the devil. You need to get on Satan's case!

Many times I've suffered from things and just tried to believe God and go on. Because I was busy and had other things to do, I just ignored it. Eventually though, the situation just reached a place where I couldn't take it anymore. I'd had all I was going to take. So I got mad, went somewhere, shut the door, and let the devil have it. "I'm through with this. It's over!" Right after that—BOOM—my miracle happened.

Then I would wonder, *Why in the world did I wait so long? Why didn't I do this earlier? Why did I go through all this if that's all I had to do?* I had lost my anger and given place to the devil. Satan is just a squatter who will stick around in your life until you evict him. You need to stir yourself up and get this Elijah attitude—*Lord, You've spoken some things to me. I have a word from You. If things look tough, I'll just pour some extra water on my sacrifice to prove You can do it! I'm going to pursue my enemy until I absolutely destroy him! Glory to Jesus!*

Don't just chase your enemy over the hill. Don't just fight until you get some relief and you can live with the rest. No! Pursue until you conquer. Make it so your enemy can never fight again. That's what Elijah did.

Chapter Twelve

Elijah Saw

"And Elijah said unto Ahab, Get thee up, eat and drink; for there is a sound of abundance of rain" (1 Kings 18:41). At the exact moment Elijah uttered these words, this "sound of abundance of rain" was only in his heart. There wasn't anything going on yet out in the physical realm. Elijah just saw it and heard it in his heart.

Violently Resolved

"So Ahab went up to eat and to drink. And Elijah went up to the top of Carmel; and he cast himself down upon the earth, and put his face between his knees. And said to his servant, Go up now, look toward the sea. And he went up, and looked, and said, There is nothing. And he said, Go again seven times. And it came to pass at the seventh time, that he said, Behold, there ariseth a little cloud out of the sea, like a man's hand. And he said, Go up, say unto Ahab, Prepare thy chariot, and get thee down that the rain stop thee not" (1 Kings 18:42-44). Elijah didn't pray seven times—he only prayed once. Even though he sent his servant to go look seven times, he only prayed once.

"Elias **[Elijah]** was a man subject to like passions as we are, and he prayed earnestly that it might not rain: and it rained not on the earth by the space of three years and six months. And he prayed again, and the heaven gave rain, and the earth brought forth her fruit" (James 5:17-18; brackets mine). Sometimes people think it's wrong to pray about something more than once, but Scripture tells us we ought to "pray without ceasing" (1 Thessalonians 5:17). I don't believe this scripture is saying to pray twenty-four hours a day. I'm not praying right now—I'm writing. There are times when you're speaking, singing, etc., but not really praying. And you can't pray when you're asleep. Praying without ceasing simply means not to stop praying until you see what you've prayed for manifest.

According to James, Elijah prayed one prayer but he sent his servant out seven times. It was just one prayer, but it was a continual prayer. Elijah kept praying—he prayed without ceasing—until he saw the answer manifest. He became violently resolved.

One Awesome Day

At first, all Elijah's servant saw was a cloud the size of a man's hand. When I was on top of Mount Carmel, it was a clear day. I remember looking out toward the Mediterranean and seeing a tiny, tiny cloud about the size of a man's hand. It couldn't have been more perfect. I looked at that and thought, *Elijah had to have faith to believe a three-year drought would end by seeing a cloud that small!*

"And it came to pass in the mean while, that the heaven was black with clouds and wind, and there was a great rain. And Ahab rode, and went to Jezreel. And the hand of the LORD was on Elijah; and he girded up his loins **[pulled up and tucked in his robe]**, and ran before Ahab to the entrance of Jezreel" (1 Kings 18:45-46; brackets mine). Basically, Elijah outran Ahab almost twenty miles, even though Ahab had a head start and a chariot. Elijah was pumped! He had just mocked and killed the 850 prophets of Baal and the groves, called down fire from heaven, and prayed and ended a three-year drought. Elijah's adrenaline was pumping so hard that he outran a chariot twenty miles and beat Ahab to Jezreel. This was an awesome day in the life of Elijah!

Drenched in Blood

But let's look in chapter 19. "And Ahab told Jezebel all that Elijah had done, and withal how he had slain all the prophets with the sword. Then Jezebel sent a messenger unto Elijah, saying, So let the gods do to me, and more also, if I make not thy life as the life of one of them by tomorrow about this time" (1 Kings 19:1-2). Queen Jezebel was the one who had fed all of these false "prophets." Since they ate at her table (1 Kings 18:19), this meant it was a state religion. She had totally rejected God.

She had brought in the prophets of Baal, the prophets of the groves, and subsidized them, fed them, and took care of them.

They were her prophets. It was her religion. And she didn't do Elijah the honor of even showing up on Mount Carmel when the whole nation was called together. I'm sure she did that just to spite him. Jezebel didn't like Elijah because he was a prophet of the Lord.

Upon hearing the news of all Elijah had done, she became furious and took an oath saying, "May the gods make me like one of these slaughtered prophets if Elijah isn't dead by this time tomorrow!" Then she sent a messenger to tell Elijah what she was determined to do. "And when he **[Elijah]** saw that, he arose, and went **[fled]** for his life" (1 Kings 19:3; brackets mine).

What did Elijah see when he received this message from Jezebel? He had just killed 850 people. We usually tend to skim over this because it isn't real pleasant, but we need to stop and envision it. Elijah killed 850 people with a sword. He did it. Can you imagine that? That's a huge pile of corpses! Think of the blood that Elijah must have been drenched in. What a graphic scene Jezebel's words must have brought to Elijah's mind!

Temptation Follows Success

So what did Elijah see? He saw himself like one of those dead men he had just slaughtered. Jezebel painted a word picture, "So let the gods do to me, and more also, if you aren't like one of those dead prophets by this time tomorrow!" Elijah's mind flashed back to that grisly scene and he saw himself dead. That's why he fled.

The day before, he had seen the word God had put in his heart. He saw himself challenging the prophets of Baal to a duel, calling down fire, and slaughtering them. He told the Lord, "Let the people know that I have done these things at Your word." He had seen these things already in his heart. He saw and heard the sound of abundance of rain when there wasn't any evidence yet in the natural realm.

However, this same ability to see what God says on the inside can work in reverse. You can see both positive and negative things in your heart. The truth is that most of us tend to see the negative. Elijah saw himself dead, which is why he fled. Although Jezebel desired to kill Elijah, she didn't have the power to do it. If she had, she wouldn't have sent a messenger with a note. She would have sent a soldier with a sword. If Jezebel had truly intended to kill Elijah at that moment, she would have done so without warning him.

In reality, Jezebel was trying to intimidate Elijah. Ahab attempted the same thing in chapter 18, but Elijah rejected it. Your greatest temptations will often come immediately after your greatest victories.

Vulnerable in Prosperity

Success is harder to handle than failure. Although this is true, most people don't believe it. They say, "What's really inside you comes out when you're squeezed." Actually, it's just the opposite. Your true character is revealed in times of success. When you're under the gun and it looks like you're going to die, it's an easy time to seek the Lord. When everything is bad and you're under pressure, you know there's no other option. Unless God comes through, you're in big trouble. Most people who have any commitment, any relationship with the Lord, will seek Him during hard times.

But where most people are destroyed is in prosperity. You'll find out what's really in someone when there isn't any pressure on, when everything is going fine and it looks like it's going to continue that way forever. You can tell more about a person's character in prosperity than you can in adversity.

When everything is going good, we tend not to be as God-dependent. That's why we're the most vulnerable in the midst of prosperity. We tend to become more self-reliant when things are going well. That is exactly what happened to Elijah.

Chapter Thirteen

"Better than My Fathers"

"And when he saw that, he arose, and went for his life, and came to Beersheba, which belongeth to Judah, and left his servant there. But he himself went a day's journey into the wilderness, and came and sat down under a juniper tree: and he requested for himself that he might die; and said, It is enough; now, O LORD, take away my life; for I am not better than my fathers" (1 Kings 19:3-4).

If Elijah really wanted to die, all he had to do was stay there and Jezebel would oblige him. The same is true for so many of us. We get into self-pity and say things like, "Nothing ever works for me. Things never turn out right!" But we know in our hearts that what we're saying isn't true. Elijah was praying, "Take away my life," when the truth was he didn't really want to die. He was in self-pity.

Here is a revealing statement: "O LORD, take away my life; for I am not better than my fathers" (1 Kings 19:4). This says a lot! Elijah had been thinking that he was better than his fathers. He had done things that nobody else had ever done. He had called for a drought, which had never happened before. There had been droughts, but not a God-called drought where He used someone as an instrument to begin and end it.

No one had ever ended a drought the way Elijah did. In fact, no one had multiplied food, raised somebody from the dead, called down fire from heaven, turned an entire nation to God, or outran a chariot in all of history like Elijah did. He had just experienced an unbroken string of successes. This was dangerous territory, as he started thinking that he was better than his fathers.

Intimidated

Even though he heard this report from Obadiah in chapter 18, that there were still a hundred of the Lord's prophets being hid in a cave and fed, Elijah said, "I, even I only, remain a prophet of the Lord" (1 Kings 18:22). How did Elijah come up with that? Either he chose to ignore what Obadiah had said or he thought, *Well, they aren't prophets like I am. Nobody is serving God like me!*

Jezebel wanted to kill Elijah, but she was like any other ruler. She didn't really have the power to just snuff him out. If she did, she wouldn't have sent a messenger with a note. She would have sent a soldier with a sword. If she really wanted to kill Elijah, she would have killed him. She wouldn't have warned him. In reality, she was trying to intimidate him.

Ahab tried to intimidate Elijah in 1 Kings 18:17, but he rejected it. But in this instance with Jezebel, he failed and fled. Why? Because Elijah honestly thought that somehow or another,

God was using him because of some superior ability, quality, or characteristic in his life. He thought he was better than other people. The moment you believe that, you're headed for trouble.

Elijah's Downfall

Elijah began by being God dependent. He started out totally trusting and relying on God to do things through him. But somewhere along the way, as he saw his successes, he actually moved his identity and confidence away from who he was in the Lord and what God had done in him. His identity and confidence shifted to himself and to what he had done.

This isn't hard to do. It's easy to be God dependent when you're struggling, things aren't going good, and there's nothing you can see in the natural upon which to base your faith. The only thing you can hang your faith on is the word God has given you.

But when you start seeing success and things begin to work, many people move their confidence away from the Lord and what He has said, to things they can see. Then they believe they're a success because of the size of their church, the income of their ministry, the miracles they have seen, or something else. The moment they do that, they just transferred their confidence and dependency from God to something else. Although this is something many people don't want to face, sooner or later every minister—every ministry—will experience problems. It doesn't matter who you are.

Elijah fell because he transferred his faith and confidence from the Lord to himself. That's why he failed. And this is true for every last one of us. Whenever we fail and experience these difficulties, one way or another we have done this same exact thing. Don't just wait and experience this truth for yourself. Learn this lesson at Elijah's expense. Transferring your faith and confidence from God to yourself is deadly.

Elijah was so strong that he had defied the king, his armies, and all the prophets of Baal. He stood there and mocked them in front of the entire nation, saying, "Maybe your god is asleep. Yell louder!" He did all of those things, including killing 850 people. Yet, one woman with a note caused him to flee in terror. Why? Elijah had taken his faith and confidence away from the Lord and put it upon himself and the things he had done. Elijah's strength was supposed to be in the Lord, not in himself. This is true for every one of us.

Your Flesh Is Capable

I'm amazed how many people think that the longer we're with the Lord, the stronger and more anointed we become. We think somehow or another that *we're* improving in the process. The truth is the exact opposite. If we are seeing a greater manifestation of God in our lives—greater joy, power, freedom, and so forth—the truth is we are becoming more and more dependent *on Him*.

Even though we are more focused on God and can hear Him better, our flesh never improves. Our flesh is still flesh. And the moment we get out of the spirit and into the flesh, we are as capable of doing anything as our flesh ever was capable of doing.

A pastor friend of mine loved God and good things were happening in his life. However, he fell into a problem and became so discouraged that he threw his Bible out the window and went back to taking drugs. He attempted suicide and wound up in the psychiatric ward of a hospital in Colorado Springs.

Don Krow and I went to visit him, but he wouldn't let us in. Even though he was a good friend of ours, he was too embarrassed to see us. We forced our way in anyway, and found him just sitting there crying. He told us, "I can't believe I did this! I love God. I've pastored a church. I know better. How could I have done something like this?"

When you get out of the spirit and into the flesh, your flesh is as capable of doing anything as it ever was. It's like flying an airplane. As long as the engines are running, the plane is flying, and you're in it and doing great. But if you step out of that airplane, it doesn't matter who you are — you're going down! It wasn't you keeping yourself in the air. It was the vehicle you were riding in that was propelling you and giving you this ability to fly. Once you step out of that vehicle, you're on your own.

It's the same with God. We somehow or another think, *God, I've really become strong now. I'm greater than I used to be. I'm different than I used to be!* No, your flesh is exactly the same as it ever was. The only victory you're experiencing is because you've become more and more God-dependent. You've let Him live through you

(Galatians 2:20). The moment you quit letting God live through you by getting back into self-centeredness and self-sufficiency, you are as capable of doing anything as you ever were.

Headed for Failure

It's dangerous for people to experience success who don't have the character to handle it. That's one reason many of us haven't really experienced very much success yet. God is more concerned about us than He is about our ministry. He's more concerned about us than He is concerned with just using us. God won't promote us if He knows we can't handle it, because He knows that we will be destroyed.

God loves you! Even though He may have given you a call and you can see what the vision is, there is a time in between receiving the call, being separated to that call, and then seeing the fulfillment of it. We're the ones, primarily, who dictate this time frame based on what kind of character we develop on the inside.

This is exactly what happened to Elijah. He never was better than his fathers. When he called fire down from heaven, it wasn't because of his holiness or ability. It was because he was dependent on God and looking totally to Him. As soon as Elijah started reading his own press releases, he swelled up in pride. He was headed for failure the moment he thought, *I've done things nobody else has ever done. I'm special!* It just so happened that the woman with the note triggered his collapse. However, the inevitable could have happened some other way. What an amazing truth!

Chapter Fourteen

"What Are You Doing Here?"

"And as he lay and slept under a juniper tree, behold, then an angel touched him, and said unto him, Arise and eat. And he looked, and, behold, there was a cake baken on the coals, and a cruse of water at his head. And he did eat and drink, and laid him down again. And the angel of the LORD came again the second time, and touched him, and said, Arise and eat; because the journey is too great for thee. And he arose, and did eat and drink, and went in the strength of that meat forty days and forty nights unto Horeb the mount of God. And he came thither unto a cave, and lodged there; and, behold, the word of the LORD came to him, and he said unto him, What doest thou here, Elijah?" (1 Kings 19:5-9). God asked Elijah, "What are you doing here?" Elijah wasn't "there." This wasn't where God wanted him to be. They were having a revival in Samaria, but the guy God used to spark it had fled. Instead of rejoicing and leading the people, Elijah was hiding and complaining.

Within forty-eight hours or so of seeing the fire of God fall, slaughtering the false prophets, and praying down rain, this guy was so discouraged and depressed that he was telling God to kill him. So the Lord asked, "What are you doing here? This isn't "there!" This is not where I want you to be."

Excuses, Excuses

Look at Elijah's answer. "And he said, I have been very jealous for the LORD God of hosts: for the children of Israel have forsaken thy covenant, thrown down thine altars, and slain thy prophets with the sword; and I, even I only, am left; and they seek my life, to take it away" (1 Kings 19:10). Lie! That was a lie! Instead of humbling himself, he justified himself. Elijah was defeated, depressed, and in retreat, but he still wasn't willing to admit, *God, it's me. I missed it.* Instead, he was contending, *It's other people and what they've done. I'm the only one left!*

This attitude is prevalent in our society today. Very few people accept responsibility for themselves and their actions. They blame anything and everything else. I've heard all kinds of excuses as I've traveled. Normally, the people start telling me how hard it is to minister saying, "Nobody can make it here. This is the occult capital of the United States." Really? I've been to at least a hundred places that claimed that distinction.

They will say, "But you don't understand. They're all snowbirds down here. They're here to retire and get away from everything. They aren't seeking God!" They always have the excuse that because of something or somebody else, their church isn't growing or nothing is working. They say, "It's those people!" or they use the old standby, "It's that woman who You gave me!" We're always using some excuse.

"I'm the Only One!"

That's exactly what Elijah was doing. He was sitting there saying, "God, I've been jealous for You. I've done good. It wasn't me. It was these people. I'm the only one left!" That wasn't the right answer. The Lord was giving him a test to see if he had repented, but he gave the wrong answer.

Elijah was deceived. He was saying, "I'm the only one serving You!" Any time you think you're the only one serving God, you can just write "Ichabod" over your head (1 Samuel 4:21-22). The glory has departed! Never, under any circumstances, are you ever the only one who loves God. You are never the only person in your city or church serving Him. Any time you think that, you're in big trouble. It's just never, ever true.

Elijah knew differently. He knew that there were other prophets still living and serving God (1 Kings 18:13). But apparently, he had written them off saying, "They aren't of my caliber. They aren't 'full Gospel.' They don't have the revelation. I'm the only one preaching the true word of God." That's a terrible attitude!

The Still, Small Voice

So the Lord spoke to Elijah again. "And he said, Go forth, and stand upon the mount before the LORD. And, behold, the LORD passed by, and a great and strong wind rent the mountains, and brake in pieces the rocks before the LORD; but the LORD was not in the wind: and after the wind an earthquake; but the LORD was not in the earthquake: And after the earthquake a fire; but the LORD was not in the fire: and after the fire a still small voice" (1 Kings 19:11-12).

Elijah had started off just listening to the still small voice and having a relationship with God. He was a "nobody." No one knew him. Nothing dramatic had ever happened. Then the Lord spoke a word into his heart concerning a drought, and the ball started rolling.

Later on, Elijah saw God do so many powerful things through him that he moved away from the simple and got into the spectacular. He moved away from being intimate with and completely dependent on God. It can be hard to handle seeing fire fall from heaven, consume the sacrifice, and spark a great revival. What do you do for an encore?

I've met many ministers who have seen God use them in great manifestations of His power. However, in a sense, it ruins them. They become bored after that. After awhile, that little zing, that emotional high you get from being somebody special, wears off. Then you have to do something else to become someone special again. It's easy to transfer your dependence and faith away from God and onto things.

The Lord sent the awesome wind, earthquake, and fire—all of these dramatic, spectacular things—but He wasn't in any of them.

God manifested Himself to Elijah in the still, small voice. The Lord was calling Elijah back to humility and intimate relationship. He was saying, "Elijah, you've gotten away from this. This was what made you who you are. It's what made the things you've seen happen. Yet, you've gotten away from them."

Re-Tested

When Elijah first started his ministry, he had nothing in the natural going for him—except he had a word from God. Because of this, he was dependent on God and spent time just loving and worshiping Him. Then Elijah became a success. He saw God use him in ways that even Moses wasn't used. He moved away from the simplicity of his relationship with the Lord. He left his first love (Revelation 2:4).

In 1 Kings 19:11-12, the Lord did all those dramatic things, but He wasn't in them. He was in the still, small voice. You'll never grow beyond this. You'll never grow beyond this personal, intimate relationship with God. This must be the foundation for anyone who is going to stay with God over a prolonged period of time. It was this humility and intimacy with the Lord that Elijah had gotten away from. Yet, he was still mightily used of God.

In verse 13, the Lord finally spoke to Elijah in a still, small voice saying, "What are you doing here, Elijah?" God asked him the same question He had asked before (1 Kings 19:9). As you know, the Lord doesn't repeat Himself often. He'll say something to you, and then you won't hear from Him again until you deal with what He said before. It's pretty serious when God repeats Himself.

Elijah had failed the first test. God had asked, "What are you doing here, Elijah?" Instead of humbling himself and saying, "I got into pride and thought I was better than everyone else," he blamed everybody else saying, "I've been faithful. I'm the only one!" Elijah failed the first time, so God let him take the test over again by asking the same question. However, Elijah answered with the same exact words!

Pride and Arrogance

"And he said, I have been very jealous for the LORD God of hosts: because the children of Israel have forsaken thy covenant, thrown down thine altars, and slain thy prophets with the sword; and I, even I only, am left; and they seek my life, to take it away" (1 Kings 19:14). This wasn't true the first time, and it wasn't true the second time either. If the Lord lets you retake a test, it's because you failed the first time around. Elijah should have at least tried a different answer.

The Lord finally went on and said, "There are seven thousand who haven't bowed the knee to Baal" (1 Kings 19:18). Elijah knew of at least a hundred, but there were SEVEN THOUSAND who were still faithful servants of God. Any time you think you're the only person with a revelation or who's doing something, you're wrong! You've moved into some form of pride and arrogance, thinking that you have something nobody else has. It's never true.

The Lord then told Elijah to do three things. One was to get a replacement—to find Elisha and anoint him to be prophet in his stead. Personally, I don't believe Elisha was God's original plan.

Plan "B"

David wasn't God's first choice either. "And Samuel said to Saul, Thou hast done foolishly: thou hast not kept the commandment of the LORD thy God, which he commanded thee: for now would the LORD have established thy kingdom upon Israel for ever. But now thy kingdom shall not continue: the LORD hath sought him a man after his own heart, and the LORD hath commanded him to be captain over his people, because thou hast not kept that which the LORD commanded thee" (1 Samuel 13:13-14).

Samuel told Saul, "If you would have humbled yourself today, God would have established your throne in Israel forever." Saul was God's first choice. He wasn't an intermediate step on the way to David. There never would have been a David if Saul had been faithful. Saul was God's first choice and he blew it! David was God's second choice. Although David worked out great and God's Plan "B" was better than we could imagine Plan "A" would have been, who knows what would have happened if Saul would have been faithful and stayed true to God?

I believe it's the same thing here. Elijah, not Elisha, was God's real choice in this matter. Elisha simply fulfilled what Elijah was called to do. If Elijah had remained faithful—humbled himself and given the right response to God's questioning—he would have finished his work. The things Elisha did, Elijah would have accomplished.

"I Quit!"

Look what God told Elijah to do: "And the LORD said unto him, Go, return on thy way to the wilderness of Damascus: and when thou comest, anoint Hazael to be king over Syria: And Jehu the son of Nimshi shalt thou anoint to be king over Israel: and Elisha the son of Shaphat of Abelmeholah shalt thou anoint to be prophet in thy room. And it shall come to pass, that him that escapeth the sword of Hazael shall Jehu slay: and him that escapeth from the sword of Jehu shall Elisha slay. Yet I have left me seven thousand in Israel, all the knees which have not bowed unto Baal, and every mouth which hath not kissed him" (1 Kings 19:15-18).

Upon hearing these words, Elijah immediately departed and did the last thing he was commanded to do. He anointed Elisha to be prophet in his stead. Elijah never did the other two things God had told him to do. Elisha had to do them instead (2 Kings 8:7-15; 9:1-11). Elisha wouldn't have done them if Elijah had.

After several powerful manifestations of wind, earthquake, and fire, here was the Lord speaking to Elijah in a still, small, audible voice. God gave him three specific things to do, but Elijah just skipped over two-thirds of the instructions. He went right away and anointed his successor, which was like saying, "I'm ready to get out of this. I'm ready to die." Basically, Elijah anointed his successor and quit.

There were only a few things recorded of Elijah in Scripture after this. When Ahab killed Naboth (1 Kings 21:1-16), Elijah went down and prophesied destruction over Ahab and Jezebel (1 Kings 21:17-24). Then Ahab's son, Ahaziah, sent soldiers to kill him in 2 Kings 1. Elijah simply called down fire from heaven and consumed 102 men. However, this wasn't God's perfect will. Jesus rebuked His disciples in the New Testament for trying to do the same thing (Luke 9:54-56). If Christ had physically been there in 2 Kings, He would have rebuked Elijah too. I'm not saying Elijah sinned, but it was never God's best.

Chapter Fifteen

Be Faithful!

After Elijah anointed Elisha, he didn't do very much. This was basically the end of his ministry. Elijah never anointed the two kings God had commanded him to anoint. What Ahab did to Naboth was totally unjust. He wanted Naboth's vineyard but Naboth wouldn't sell, so Jezebel and Ahab set him up and brought false charges against him. After Jezebel had Naboth stoned, she told Ahab to go down and possess his vineyard (1 Kings 21).

If Elijah had been obedient to anoint Jehu as king, Ahab and Jezebel wouldn't have done this. When Elisha did finally anoint him, Jehu marched right out of the room, rode straight into Samaria, and immediately killed Ahaziah, Jezebel, and all of Ahab's relatives (2 Kings 9-10). Ahab had already died in battle some time before (1 Kings 22:34-40).

As Jehu took over the kingdom, he deceived all of the nation's Baal worshipers into gathering together at once in the house of Baal. Then he closed the gates and ordered his army to kill every single one of them. Jehu made the house of Baal a latrine (2 Kings 10:27). He was vicious!

If Elijah had anointed Jehu as king, Ahab and Jezebel would have been dead and Naboth would never have been killed. The death of Naboth was actually a result of Elijah failing to do what God had told him to do. Therefore, Elijah was responsible for Naboth's death.

Since Scripture doesn't tell us exactly what would have or could have happened, it's not productive to speculate. However, we do know that people—both individuals and the nation as a whole—suffered because of Elijah's disobedience. Elisha was actually a second thought. All of this would probably have never happened if Elijah had fulfilled his ministry.

Called by Grace

I've heard many people testify that they weren't God's first choice for the assignment He called them to do. You may not be God's first choice either. You may be picking up a mantle that someone else laid down. You may say, "But Andrew, that's hard on my pride!" Good!

You need to recognize that God has never yet had anybody qualified working for Him. The Lord isn't using you because you're so perfect, holy, and have it all together. If you keep this in mind, it will prevent you from getting this "Elijah Syndrome" and slipping into this attitude of, *I'm the only one!*

God uses us because we're available, responsive, and fully trusting in Him. But the moment you think that the Lord is using you because of who you are and what you've done, you're headed for trouble (Proverbs 16:18). God could easily raise up somebody else to do His work instead. Although He calls you based on His grace, whether or not the Lord promotes you any further depends on how you respond to certain things.

If Elijah had humbled himself when God tested him, I believe the Lord would have restored him. Then Elijah could have fulfilled his call in life. But since he continued in arrogance, Elijah missed most of the rest of God's plan.

Stay Humble

God loves us and it's by His grace that He's called any of us to minister. It's His grace that has given us whatever gifts we have. Your gifts and callings are by grace. They aren't based on your performance (Romans 11:29). But as far as your God-given sphere of influence, it is dependent on a lot of things.

If you've proven to be a person without character, the Lord won't promote you. That doesn't mean you can't be promoted. We have a religious system today that can promote people itself. Some folks who make it to the top, who get on radio and television and become famous, were not put there by God. The Lord doesn't promote someone who isn't going to accurately represent Him.

If you fall into this "Elijah Syndrome" and flunk your test, humble yourself and learn from your mistakes. If God gives you a retest and you continue in your arrogance, you could actually decrease your influence and cut your ministry short. Faithfulness is important. God rewards faithfulness. He has a perfect plan for every single one of us, totally independent of our performance. However, your ability to experience and fulfill that plan will depend on how closely you follow the Lord and stay humble before Him.

Elijah was a man who did all these great things. But he also failed—big time! When God spoke to him in an audible voice, Elijah refused to do two-thirds of what He commanded him to do. Yet, Elijah walked with God to such a degree that he was translated into heaven. He was one of only two people who never died (2 Kings 2:11; Hebrews 11:5). Talk about grace!

Know Your Place

Basically, Elijah never fulfilled his ministry. He didn't do everything God had told him to do. He quit midstream because he failed. Elijah was never able to recover and get back on track because his confidence was in himself. Yet, he walked with God to such a degree that he was translated.

"And it came to pass, when the LORD would take up Elijah into heaven by a whirlwind, that Elijah went with Elisha from Gilgal. And Elijah said unto Elisha, Tarry here, I pray thee; for the LORD hath sent me to Bethel. And Elisha said unto him, As the LORD liveth, and as thy soul liveth, I will not leave thee. So they went down to Bethel. And Elijah said unto him, Elisha, tarry here, I pray thee; for the LORD hath sent me to Jericho. And he said,

As the LORD liveth, and as thy soul liveth, I will not leave thee. So they came to Jericho. And Elijah said unto him, Tarry, I pray thee, here: for the LORD hath sent me to Jordan. And he said, As the LORD liveth, and as thy soul liveth, I will not leave thee. And they two went on" (2 Kings 2:1-2, 4, 6).

Elijah tried to part with Elisha three different times, but Elisha just held on. Elisha had this concept that Elijah possessed in the beginning: He was going to be where God wanted him to be. He was going to be "there." Elisha knew what was going to happen to Elijah, and he refused to stay "here." He went "there." He knew his place was with Elijah, not somewhere else. Therefore, he wouldn't take "no" for an answer. Elisha was a faithful guy.

Fully Dependent on Him

Elisha was never rebuked the way Elijah was. We didn't see the failure in Elisha's life the way we saw it in Elijah's. Elisha performed twice as many miracles, yet he wasn't translated. He died. In fact, the Scripture records that he died sick. "Now Elisha was fallen sick of his sickness whereof he died…And Elisha died, and they buried him. And the bands of the Moabites invaded the land at the coming in of the year. And it came to pass, as they were burying a man, that, behold, they spied a band of men; and they cast the man into the sepulchre of Elisha: and when the man was let down, and touched the bones of Elisha, he revived, and stood up on his feet" (2 Kings 13:14, 20-21).

Even though Elisha died of sickness, the power of God operated so strongly in him that a dead man came back to life after merely touching his bones! I don't understand how there was enough anointing in Elisha's bones to raise the dead, yet he died of sickness. I also don't understand how Elisha could be more faithful than Elijah, yet not have the same results. Why wasn't he translated, too? Apparently, there were other variables that we're not aware of.

There is much to learn from the life of Elijah. When you begin to see success and start feeling like you've done something, you better draw near to God and keep your full dependence on Him. If you swell up in pride, you will be headed for a fall (Proverbs 16:18). Recognize that you aren't the only one preaching the Word, ministering in power, and doing something to advance God's kingdom. You need to maintain a humble attitude. If you do, the Lord will be able to preserve you from the kinds of problems we saw in the life of Elijah (1 Peter 5:5-6).

Conclusion

Hopefully, the Lord has used this book to teach you many things from the life of Elijah, things that will have a direct impact on you and your relationship with Him. Here is a summary of some of the major points in this book.

1. Any person who has a word from God has the potential to change his or her world.

2. You have to be faithful to act on the first word the Lord gives you before you will get any more words from Him.

3. God sends His provision to where He told you to go, not to where you are. There is a place called "there" for me and you.

4. Our place called "there" isn't a static place; it changes. We must maintain our relationship with the Lord to detect the change.

5. Elijah wasn't taking from the widow when he asked for her last bit of food. He was God's instrument to provide her with food for years, and to enable her to see her son raised from the dead. Likewise, when I receive offerings I'm not taking from people, I'm helping them receive from God.

6. I have been challenged by Elijah's boldness with Ahab and the prophets of Baal. He didn't just resist them; he destroyed them.

7. I've also been inspired by Elijah's mistakes. Elijah was intimidated by a messenger with a note, not a soldier with a sword. This happened because he saw himself dead. He quit looking at things through the eyes of God's Word.

8. I have learned that after great success, comes great temptation for us to get into pride. Elijah thought he was better than his fathers. Success is a greater temptation than hardship.

9. Elijah told the Lord he was the only one serving Him, although he knew that wasn't true. He was going by his emotions, instead of the truth. This always leads to disaster.

10. Elijah was looking for God in some dramatic, supernatural way, but God manifested Himself in a still, small voice. We can miss God if we are only looking for some spectacular manifestation.

11. When God gave Elijah a second chance on his test, Elijah gave the same wrong answer. If he wanted to get a different result, he should have given a different answer. If we don't like the grade we receive, we need to do something different.

12. God spoke to Elijah in an audible voice telling him to do three things, yet Elijah chose not to do two of them. He only obeyed the third command, which was to anoint

Elisha as his replacement. Elijah never fulfilled all God told him to do. God help me not to make this same mistake.

13. Despite Elijah's failures, he still walked with God to the degree that he didn't die. He was taken up into heaven in a whirlwind. This gives hope to me and to all who have ever missed God, that we can still have a powerful relationship with the Lord. God is full of grace.

As I shared at the beginning of this book, we don't have to learn all of life's lessons through our own hard knocks. This is why the Lord gave us the good, the bad, and the ugly of so many Bible character's lives, so we can learn by their mistakes.

I pray that the Holy Spirit uses the things I've pointed out in this book about the life of Elijah to inspire you, while warning you about Satan's plots against your life. The devil doesn't have any new tricks. He just recycles the same old stuff he's been using throughout history. There is nothing he can do to you that isn't common to all men (1 Corinthians 10:13). We can overcome just as Elijah overcame—with the Word of God.

Receive Jesus as Your Savior

Choosing to receive Jesus Christ as your Lord and Savior is the most important decision you'll ever make!

God's Word promises, "That if thou shalt confess with thy mouth the Lord Jesus, and shalt believe in thine heart that God hath raised him from the dead, thou shalt be saved. For with the heart man believeth unto righteousness; and with the mouth confession is made unto salvation" (Romans 10:9,10). "For whosoever shall call upon the name of the Lord shall be saved" (Romans 10:13).

By His grace, God has already done everything to provide salvation. Your part is simply to believe and receive.

Pray out loud: Jesus, I confess that You are my Lord and Savior. I believe in my heart that God raised You from the dead. By faith in Your Word, I receive salvation now. Thank You for saving me.

The very moment you commit your life to Jesus Christ, the truth of His Word instantly comes to pass in your spirit. Now that you're born again, there's a brand-new you.

Receive the Holy Spirit

As His child, your loving heavenly Father wants to give you the supernatural power you need to live a new life.

> *For every one that asketh receiveth; and he that seeketh findeth; and to him that knocketh it shall be opened...how much more shall your heavenly Father give the Holy Spirit to them that ask him?*
>
> *Luke 11:10-13*

All you have to do is ask, believe, and receive!

Pray: *Father, I recognize my need for Your power to live a new life. Please fill me with Your Holy Spirit. By faith, I receive it right now. Thank You for baptizing me. Holy Spirit, You are welcome in my life.*

Congratulations—now you're filled with God's supernatural power.

Some syllables from a language you don't recognize will rise up from your heart to your mouth. (1 Corinthians 14:14) As you speak them out loud by faith, you're releasing God's power from within and building yourself up in the spirit. (1 Corinthians 14:4) You can do this whenever and wherever you like.

It doesn't really matter whether you felt anything or not when you prayed to receive the Lord and His Spirit. If you believed in your heart that you received, then God's Word promises you did. "Therefore I say unto you, What things soever ye desire, when ye pray, believe that ye receive them, and ye shall have them" (Mark 11:24). God always honors His Word—believe it!

Please contact me and let me know that you've prayed to receive Jesus as your Savior or be filled with the Holy Spirit. I would like to rejoice with you and help you understand more fully what has taken place in your life. I'll send you a free gift that will help you understand and grow in your new relationship with the Lord. Welcome to your new life!

About the Author

For over four decades, Andrew Wommack has traveled America and the world teaching the truth of the Gospel. His profound revelation of the Word of God is taught with clarity and simplicity, emphasizing God's unconditional love and the balance between grace and faith. He reaches millions of people through the daily *Gospel Truth* radio and television programs, broadcast both domestically and internationally. He founded Charis Bible College in 1994 and has since established CBC extension schools in other major cities of America and around the world. Andrew has produced a library of teaching materials, available in print, audio, and visual formats. And, as it has been from the beginning, his ministry continues to distribute free audio materials to those who cannot afford them.

Charis Bible College

Combining the rich teaching of God's Word with practical ministry experience.

You have a destiny!
Find it at Charis.

Over 70 campuses across the U.S. and around the world

Convenient distance-learning options

Start down the path to your destiny.

Visit **www.CharisBibleCollege.org** to see all our program options, or call 719-635-6029.

To contact Andrew Wommack please write, e-mail, or call:

Andrew Wommack Ministries, Inc.
P.O. Box 3333
Colorado Springs, CO 80934-3333
E-mail: awommack@aol.com
Helpline Phone (orders and prayer):
719-635-1111
Hours: 4:00 AM to 9:30 PM MST

Andrew Wommack Ministries of Europe
P.O. Box 4392
WS1 9AR Walsall
England
E-mail: enquiries@awme.net
U.K. Helpline Phone (orders and prayer):
011-44-192-247-3300
Hours: 5:30 AM to 4:00 PM GMT

Or visit him on the Web at: www.awmi.net